Cotton Mather, James Janeway

A Token for Children

Being an exact account of the conversion, holy and exemplary lives and joyful

deaths of several young children

Cotton Mather, James Janeway

A Token for Children

Being an exact account of the conversion, holy and exemplary lives and joyful deaths of several young children

ISBN/EAN: 9783337105822

Printed in Europe, USA, Canada, Australia, Japan

Cover: Foto ©ninafisch / pixelio.de

More available books at **www.hansebooks.com**

A TOKEN FOR CHILDREN,

BEING

An Exact Account of the Conversion, Holy and Exemplary Lives and Joyful Deaths of several YOUNG-CHILDREN.

BY

JAMES JANEWAY,

MINISTER OF THE GOSPEL.

To which is added,

A TOKEN for the CHILDREN of

NEW-ENGLAND,

OR,

Some Examples of CHILDREN, in whom the Fear of GOD was remarkably Budding before they died; in several Parts of NEW-ENGLAND.

Preserved and Published for the Encouragement of *PIETY* in other Children.

WITH NEW ADDITIONS.

BOSTON:

Printed and Sold by Z. FOWLE, in BACK-STREET, near the *Mill-Bridge.* 1771

To all Parents, School-Masters and School-Mistresses, or any who have any Hand in the Education of Children.

DEAR FRIENDS,

I *Have often thought that* Christ *speaks to you, as* Pharoah's Daughter *did to* Moses's Mother, *Take this Child and Nurse it for me.* O *Sirs, consider, what a precious Jewel is committed to your Charge, what an Advantage you have to shew your Love to* Christ, *to stock the next Generation with noble Plants, and what a joyful Account you may make if you be faithful: Remember Souls,* Christ *and Grace cannot be overvalued. I confess you have some Disadvantages, but let that only excite your Diligence; the Salvation of Souls, the Commendation of your Master, the Greatness of your Reward and everlasting Glory, will pay for all. Remember the Devil is at work hard, wicked Ones are industrious, and corrupt Nature is a rugged knotty Piece to hew. But be not discouraged, I am almost as much afraid of your Laziness and Unfaithfulness as any Thing. Do but fall to work lustily, and who knows but that rough Stone may prove a Pillar in the Temple of God? In the Name of the living* GOD, *as you will answer it shortly at his Bar, I command you to be faithful in Instructing and Catechising your young Ones. If you think I am too peremptory, I pray read the Command from my Master himself,* Deut. 6. 7. *Is not the Duty clear? and are you neglect so direct a Command? Are the Souls of your Children of no Value? Are you willing that they should be Brands of Hell? Are you indifferent whether they be damned or saved? Shall the Devil run away with them without Controul? Will not you use your utmost Endeavour to deliver them from the Wrath to come? You see that they are not Subjects uncapable of the Grace of God. Whatever you think of them, Christ doth not slight them: They are not too Little to die; they are not too Little to go to Hell; they are not too Little to serve their great Master; too Little to go to Heaven; for of such is* the Kingdom of God: *And will not a Possibility of their Conversion and Salvation, put you upon the greatest Diligence to teach them? Or are Christ and Heaven, and Salvation, small Things with you? If they be, then indeed I have done with you? But if they be not, I beseech you lay about you with all your Might: The Devil knows your Time is going apace, it will shortly be too late. O therefore what you do, do quickly, and do it, I say with all your Might: O pray, pray, pray, and live holily before them, and take some Time daily to speak a little to your Children one by one, about their miserable Condition by Nature. I knew a Child that was converted by this Sentence from a godly School-Mistress in the Country,* Every Mother's Child of you are by Nature Children of Wrath. *Put your Children upon learning their Catechism, and the Scriptures, and* etting to pray and weep by themselves after Christ: Take heed of their Company; take heed of pardoning a Lie: Take heed of letting them mispend the Sabbath. Put them I beseech you, upon imitating these sweet Children; let them read this Book over an hundred Times, and observe how they are affected, and ask them what they think of those Children, and whether they would not be such? And follow what you do with earnest Cries to God, and be in Travail to see Christ formed in their Souls. I have prayed for you, I have oft prayed for your Children, and I love them dearly; and I have prayed over these Papers; that God would strike in with them, and make them effectual to the Good of their Souls. Encourage your Children to read this Book, and lead them to improve it. What is presented, is faithfully taken from experienced solid Christians, some of them no way related to the Children, who themselves were Eye and Ear Witnesses of God's Works of Wonder, or from my own Knowledge, or from Reverend godly Ministers, and from Persons that are of unspotted Reputation for Holiness, Integrity and Wisdom; and several Passages are taken verbatim in Writing from their dying Lips. I may add many other excellent Examples, if I have Encouragement in this Piece. That the young Generation may be far more excellent than this, is the Prayer of One that dearly loves little Children.

James Janeway.

Of one eminently converted between eight and nine Years old, with an Account of her Life and Death.

MRS. *Sarah Howley*, when she was between eight and nine Years old, was carried by her Friends to hear a Sermon, where the Minister preached upon Mat. 11. 31. *My Yoke is easy and my Burden is light*: In the applying of which Scripture, this Child was mightily awakned, and made deeply sensible of the Condition of her Soul, and her Need of a CHRIST: She wept bitterly to think what a Case she was in; and went Home, and got by her self into a Chamber; and upon her Knees she wept and cry'd to the Lord, as well as she could, which might easily be perceived by her Eyes and Countenance.

2. She was not contented with this, but she got her little Brother and Sister into a Chamber with her, and told them of their Condition by Nature, and wept over them, and prayed with them and for them.

3. After this she heard another Sermon from Prov. 29. 1. *He that being often reproved, hardneth his Heart, shall suddenly be destroyed,*

and that without Remedy: At which she was more affected than before, & was so exceeding solicitous about her Soul, that she spent a great Part of the Night in weeping and praying, and could scarce take any Rest Day and Night for some Time together; desiring with all her Soul to escape from everlasting Flame, and to get an Interest in the Lord Jesus; *O what should she do for a Christ! What should she do to be saved!*

4. She gave her self much to attending upon the Word preached, and still continued very tender under it, greatly savouring what she heard.

5. She was very much in secret Prayer, as might be easily perceived by those who listened at the Chamber Door, and usually very importunate and full of Tears.

6. She could scarce speak of Sin, or be spoke to, but her Heart was ready to melt.

7. She spent much Time in reading the Scripture, and a Book called, *The best Friend in the worst of Times*; by which the Work of God was much promoted upon her Soul, and was much directed by it how to get Acquaintance with God, especially toward the End of that Book. Another Book she was much delighted with was Mr. *Swinnock's Christian Man's Calling*, and by this she was taught in this Measure to make Religion her Business. The *Spiritual Bee* was a great Companion of hers.

8. She was exceeding dutiful to her Parents, very loth to grieve them in the least : and if she had at any time (which was very rare) offended them, she would weep bitterly.

9. She abhorred Lying, and allowed herself in no known Sin.

10. She was very Conscientious in spending of Time, and hated Idleness, and spent her whole Time either in praying, reading, or instructing at her Needle, at which she was very ingenious.

11. When she was at School, she was eminent for her Diligence, Teachableness, Meekness and Modesty, speaking little ; but when she did speak, it was usually spiritual.

12. She continued in this Course of religious Duties for some Years together.

13. When she was about fourteen Years old, she brake a Vein in her Lungs (as is supposed) and oft did spit Blood, yet did a little recover again, but had several dangerous Relapses.

14. At the beginning of *January* last, she was taken very bad again, in which Sickness, she was in great distress of Soul. When she was first taken, she said, *O Mother, pray, pray, pray for me, for Satan is so busy that I cannot pray for my self ; I see I am undone without a Christ, and a Pardon ! O I am undone to all Eternity.*

15. Her Mother knowing how serious she had been formerly, did a little wonder that

she should be in such Agonies: Upon which her Mother asked her, *What Sin it was, that was so burdensome to her Spirit*: *O Mother,* said she, *It is not any particular Sin of Omission or Commission, that sticks so close to my Conscience, as the Sin of my Nature; without the Blood of Christ, that will damn me.*

16. Her Mother asked her, *What she should pray for, for her*, she answered, *That I may have a saving Knowledge of Sin and Christ, and that I may have an Assurance of God's Love to my Soul.* Her Mother asked her, *Why she did speak so little to the Minister that came to her?* She answered, *That it was her Duty with Patience and Silence to learn of them: and it was exceeding painful to her, to speak to any.*

17. One Time when she fell into a Fit, she cried out, *O I am going, I am going:* But *what shall I do to be saved? Sweet Lord Jesus, I will lie at thy Feet; and if I perish, it shall be at the Fountain of thy Mercy.*

18. She was much afraid of Presumption, and dreaded a Mistake in the Matters of her Soul, and would be often putting up Ejaculations to God, to deliver her from deceiving herself. To instance in one: *Great and mighty God, give me Faith and true Faith: Lord, That I may not be a foolish Virgin, having a Lamp and no Oil.*

19. She would many Times be laying hold upon the Promises, and plead them in Prayer. That in *Mat.* 11. 28, 29, was much on

her Tongue, and no small Relief to her Spirit. How many Times would she cry out, *Lord, Hast thou not said, Come unto me all ye that are weary and heavy laden, and I will give you rest.*

20. Another Time her Father bid her be of good Cheer, because she was going to a better Father: At which she fell into a great Passion, and said, *But how do I know that? I am a poor Sinner that wants Assurance. O, for Assurance!* It was still her Note, *O for Assurance!* This was her great, earnest, and constant Request, to all that came to her, *to beg Assurance for her:* And poor Heart, she would look with so much Eagerness upon them, as if she desired nothing in the World so much, as that they would pity her, and help her with their Prayers; never was poor Creature more earnest for any Thing, than she was for Assurance, and the Light of God's Countenance: O the piteous Moans that she would make! O the Agonies that her Soul was in!

21. Her Mother ask'd her, *If God would spare her Life, how she would live?* Truly Mother, said she, " We have such base Hearts, that I can't tell. We are apt to promise great Things when we are sick, but when we are recovered, we are as ready to forget our selves, and to return again unto Folly: but I hope I shall be more careful of my Time and my Soul than I have been."

22. She was full of natural Affection to her Parents, and very careful least her Mother

should be tired out with much watching. Her Mother said, "How shall I bear parting with thee, when I have scarce dried my Eyes for thy Brother"? She answered, "The God of Love, support and comfort you: It is but a little while, and we shall meet, I hope, in Glory." She being very weak, could speak but little, therefore her Mother said, *Child, If thou hast any Comfort, lift up thine Hand*; which she did.

23. The Lord's Day before that on which she died, a Kinsman of her's came to see her, and asking of her, whether she knew him? she replied, " Yea, I know you; and I desire you would learn to know Christ, you are Young, but you know not how soon you may die: and O, to die without a Christ, it is a fearful Thing: O redeem Time! O Time, Time, Time, precious Time"! Being requested by him not to spend her self, she said *She would do all the Good she could while she lived, and when she was dead too, as possible:* Upon which Account, she desired a Sermon might be preach'd at her Funeral, concerning the Preciousness of Time. *O that young Ones would now remember their Creator!*

24. Some Ministers that came to her, did with Earnestness beg that the Lord would please to give her some Token for Good, that she might go off triumphing; and Bills of the same Nature were sent to several Churches.

25. After she had long waited for an An-

fwer of their Prayers, fhe faid, *Well, I will venter my Soul upon Chrift.*

26. She carried it with wonderful Patience, and yet would often pray that the Lord would give her more Patience; which fhe anfwered to Aftonifhment ; for confidering the Pains and Agonies fhe was in, her Patience was next to a wonder ; *Lord, Lord, give me Patience,* faid fhe, *that I may not difhonour thee.*

27. Upon *Thurfday,* after long waiting, great Fears, and many Prayers, when all her Friends tho't fhe had been paft fpeaking, to the Aftonifhment of her Friends, fhe broke forth thus with a very audible Voice, and chearful Countenance ; " Lord, thou haft promifed, that whofoever cometh unto Thee, thou wilt in no wife caft out ; Lord, I come unto Thee ; and furely thou wilt in no wife caft me out. O fo fweet ! O fo glorious is Jefus ! O I have the fweet and glorious Jefus ; He is fweet, He is fweet, He is fweet! O the admirable Love of God in fending Chrift! O free Grace to a poor loft Creature"! And thus fhe ran on repeating many of thefe Things an hundred Times over; but her Friends were fo aftonifhed to fee her in this divine Rapture, and to hear fuch gracious Words, and her Prayers and Defires fatisfied, that they could not write a quarter of what fhe fpoke.

28. When her Soul was thus ravifhed with

the Love of Christ, and her Tongue so highly engaged in the magnifying of God; her Father, Brethren, and Sisters, with others of the Family, were called, to whom she spake particularly, as her Strength would allow. She gave her Bible as a Legacy to one of her Brothers, and desired him to use that well for her sake, and added to him, and the rest, " O make Use of Time to get a Christ for your Souls; spend no Time in running up and down in playing : O get a Christ for your Souls while you are Young. Remember now your Creator before you come to a sick Bed : Put not off this great Work 'till then, for then you will find it a hard Work indeed. I know by Experience, the Devil will tell you it is Time enough; and ye are Young, what need you to be in such haste? You will have Time enough when you are old. But there stands one *(meaning her Grandmother)* that stays behind, and I that am but young, am going before her. O therefore make your Calling and Election sure, while you are in Health. But I am afraid this will be but one Night's Trouble to your Thoughts; but remember, these are the Words of your dying Sister. O, if you knew how good Christ were ! O if you had but one Taste of his Sweetness, you would rather go to Him a thousand Times than stay in this wicked World. I would not for ten Thousand, and ten Thousand Worlds, part with my Intereſt in Chriſt. O how happy am I, that I am going to everlaſting Joys! I would not go back again for twenty Thouſand Worlds; and will you not ſtrive to get an Intereſt in Chriſt."

29. After this, looking upon one of her Father's Servants, ſhe ſaid, *What ſhall I do? What ſhall I do at the great Day, when Chriſt ſhall ſay to me,* Come thou bleſſed of my Father, inherit the Kingdom prepared for thee: *And ſhall ſay to the Wicked,* Go, thou curſed into the Lake that burns for ever. " What a Grief is it for me to think, that I ſhall ſee any of my Friends that I knew upon Earth, turned into that Lake that burns for ever! *O that Word,* For ever, *remember that,* For ever! " I ſpeak theſe Words to you, but they are nothing, except God ſpeak to you too: O pray, pray, pray, that God would give you Grace"! And then ſhe prayed, " O Lord, finiſh thy Work upon their Souls. It will be my Comfort (*ſaid ſhe*) to ſee you in Glory, but it will be your everlaſting Happineſs.

30. Her Grand-mother told her ſhe ſpent Her ſelf too much; ſhe ſaid, " I care not for that, if I could do any Soul good." O with what Vehemency did ſhe ſpeak, as if her Heart were in every Word ſhe ſpoke.

31. She was full of divine Sentences; almoſt all her Diſcourſe, from the firſt to the laſt, in the Time of her Sickneſs, was about her

t's Sweetnefs, and the Souls of
Word, like a continued Sermon.
ɔ *Friday,* after fhe had fuch lively
of God's Love, fhe was excceding
lie, and cried out, " Come Lord
quickly, conduct me to thy Ta-
am a poor Creature without Thee;
efus, my Soul longs to be with
ɹhen fhall it be? Why not now
Come Lord Jefus, come quickly;
I fpeak thus? Thy Time, dear
beſt; O give me Patience"!
ɔ *Saturday* fhe fpoke very little
drowfy) yet now and then dropt
s, " How long fweet Jefus? Fi-
rk fweet Jefus: Come away dear
Jefus, come quickly: Sweet Lord!
away, now, now, dear Jefus, come
ɔod Lord, give Patience to me to
ɔointed Time: Lord Jefus helps
:." Thus at feveral Times (when
leep) for fhe was afleep the great-
ɹe Day.
ɔ the *Lord's Day,* fhe fcarce fpoke
but much defired that Bills of
g might be fent to thofe who had
:en praying for her, that they
her to praife God for that full Af-
he had given her of his Love;
to be much fwallowed up with the
ɔf God's free Love to her Soul.
mended her Spirit into the Lord's

Hands; and the last Words she was heard to speak, were these, *Lord help, Lord Jesus help; Dear Lord Jesus; blessed Jesus*---And thus upon the Lord's Day between Nine and Ten of the Clock in the Forenoon, she slept sweetly in *Jesus,* and began an everlasting Sabbath, *February* 19, 1670.

EXAMPLE II.

Of a Child that was admirably affected with the Things of GOD, when he was between two and three Years old, with a brief Account of his Life and Death.

1. A Certain little Child, whose Mother had dedicated him to the Lord in her Womb, when he could not speak plain, would be crying after God, and was greatly desirous to be taught good Things.

2. He could not endure to be put to Bed without Family Duty, but would put his Parents upon Duty, and would with much Devotion, kneel down, and with great Patience and Delight, continue 'till Duty was at an End, without the least Expression of being weary; and he seemed never so well pleased as when he was engaged in Duty.

3. He could not be satisfied with Family Duty, but he would be oft upon his Knees by himself in one corner or other.

4. He was much delighted in hearing the Word of God, either read or preached.

5. He loved to go to School, that he might learn something of God, and would observe and take great Notice of what he had read, and come Home and speak of it with much Affection : and he would rejoice in his Book, and say to his Mother, *O Mother ! I have had a sweet Lesson to Day, will you please to give me leave to fetch my Book that you may hear it ?*

6. As he grew up, he was more and more affected with the Things of another World ; so that if we had not received our Imformation from one that is of undoubted Fidelity, it would seem incredible.

7. He quickly learned to read the Scripture, and with great Reverence, Tenderness and Groans, read 'till Tears and Sobs were ready to hinder him.

8. When he was at secret Prayer, he would weep bitterly.

9. He was won't oftentimes to complain of the naughtiness of his Heart, and seemed to be more grieved for the Corruption of his Nature, than for actual Sin.

10. He had a vast Understanding in the Things of God, even next to a Wonder, for one of his Age.

11. He was much troubled for the wandring of his Thoughts in Duty, and that he could not keep his Heart always fixed upon God, and the Work he was about, and his Affections constantly raised,

12. He kept a watch over his Heart, and obferved the workings of his Soul, and would complain that they were fo vain and foolifh, and fo little bufied about fpiritual Things.

13. As he grew up, he grew daily in Knowledge and Experience, and his Carriage was fo heavenly, and his Difcourfe fo excellent and experimental, that it made thofe which heard it, ever aftonifhed.

14. He was exceeding importunate with God in Duty ; and would plead with God at a ftrange Rate, and ufe fuch Arguments in Prayer, that one would think it were impoffible fhould ever enter into the Heart of a Child : And he would beg and expoftulate, and weep fo, that fometimes it could not be kept from the Ears of Neighbours ; fo that one of the next Houfe was forced to cry out, *The Prayers and Tears of that Child in the next Houfe will fink me to Hell, becaufe by it he did condemn his neglect of Prayer, and his flight Performance of it.*

15. He was very fearful of wicked Company, and would often beg of God to keep him from it, and that he might never be pleafed in them that took Delight in difpleafing of God : And when he was at any Time in the hearing of their wicked Words, taking the Lord's Name in vain, or Swearing, or any filthy Words, it would even make him tremble, and ready to go Home and weep.

16. He abhorred Lying with his Soul.

17. When he had committed any Sin, he

was easily convinced of it, and would get in some Corner and secret Place, and with Tears beg pardon of God, and Strength against such a Sin. He had a Friend that oft watched him, and listned at his Chamber Door, from whom I received this Narrative.

18. When he had been asked, whether he would commit such a Sin again, he would never promise absolutely, because he said his Heart was naughty; but he would weep and say, he hoped by the Grace of God he should not.

19. When he was left at Home alone upon the Sabbath Days, he would be sure not to spend any Part of the Day in Idleness and Play, but be busied in praying, reading in the Bible, and getting of his Catechism.

20. When other Children were playing, he would many a Time and oft be praying.

21. One Day a certain Person was discoursing with him, about the Nature, Offices and Excellency of Christ, and that He alone can satisfy for our Sins, and merit everlasting Life for us; and about other of the great Mysteries of Redemption; he seemed savingly to understand them, and greatly delighted with the Discourse.

22. One speaking concerning the Resurrection of the Body, he did acknowledge it; but that the same weak Body that was buried in the Church Yard shou'd be raised again, he tho't very strange, but with Admiration

yielded, that nothing was impoffible with God; and that very Day he was taken fick unto Death.

23. A Friend of his afked him, *Whether he was willing to die*, when he was firft taken fick: He anfwered *No* ; *becaufe he was afraid of his State as to another World* : Why Child, faid the other, *Thou didſt pray for a new Heart, for an humble, and ſincere Heart, and I have heard thee; didſt thou not pray with thy Heart? I hope I did,* faid he.

24. Not long after, the fame Perfon afked him again, whether he were willing to die? He anfwered, *Now I am willing, for I ſhall go to Chriſt.*

25. One afked him, *What would become of his Siſter, if he ſhould die and leave her?* He anfwered, *The Will of the Lord muſt be done.*

26. He ſtill grew weaker and weaker, but carried it with a great deal of Sweetneſs and Patience, waiting for his Change, and at laſt did chearfully commit his Spirit unto the Lord; and calling upon the Name of the Lord, and faying, *Lord Jeſus, Lord Jeſus,*---- in whofe Bofom, he fweetly ſlept, dying as I remember, when he was about five or fix Years old.

EXAMPLE III.

Of a little Girl that was wrought upon, when she was between Four and Five Years old, with some Account of her holy Life, and triumphant Death.

MAry A. when she was between four and five Years old, was greatly affected in hearing the Word of God, and became very solicitous about her Soul, and everlasting Condition, weeping bitterly to think what would become of her in another World, asking strange Questions concerning God and Christ, and her own Soul. So that this little *Mary*, before she was full five Years old, seemed to mind, *The one Thing needful*, and to choose, *The better Part*, and sat at the *Feet of Christ* many a Time, and oft with Tears.

2. She was wont to be much in secret Duty, and many times come off from her Knees with Tears.

3. She would chuse such Times and Places for secret Duty, as might render her less observed by others, and did endeavour what possible she could to conceal what she was doing when engaged in secret Duty.

4. She was greatly afraid of Hypocrisy, and of doing any Thing to be seen of Men, and to get Commendation and Praise; and when she had heard one of her Brother's saying, *That he had been by himself at Prayer*, she

rebuked him sharply, and told him, *how little such Prayers were like to profit him*, and *that it was but little to his Praise, to pray like a Hypocrite, and to be glad that any should know what he had been doing*.

5. Her Mother being full of Sorrow after the Death of her Husband, this Child came to her Mother, and ask'd her, *Why she wept so exceedingly?* Her mother answered, *She had Cause enough to weep, because her Father was dead*: *No, dear Mother*, said the Child, *you have no Cause to weep so much; for God is a good God still to you*.

6. She was a dear lover of faithful Ministers. One Time after she had been hearing of Mr. *Whitaker*, she said, *I love that Man dearly, for the sweet Words that he speaks concerning Christ*.

7. Her Book was her Delight, and what she did read, she loved to make her own, and cared not for passing over what she learned, without extraordinary Observation and Understanding; and many Times she was so strangely affected in reading of the Scriptures, that she would burst out into Tears, and would hardly be pacified, so greatly was she taken with Christ's Sufferings, the Zeal of God's Servants, and the Danger of a natural State.

8. She would complain oftentimes of the Corruption of her Nature, of the Hardness of her Heart, that she could repent no more

be no more humble and grieved
against a good God; and when
complain, it was with Abundance

s greatly concerned for the Souls
d grieved to think of the misera-
n that they were in upon this
When she could handsomely, she
tting in some pretty sweet Word
ut above all, she would do what
draw the Heart of her Brethren
after Christ: and there was no
, that her Example and good
prevail with some of them when
ry Young, to get into Corners to
ask very gracious Questions a-
ings of God.
as very consciencious in keeping
spending the whole Time either
r praying, or learning her Cate-
teaching her Brethen and Sisters.
when she was left at Home upon
ay, she got some other little Chil-
r, with her Brothers and Sisters,
f playing (as other naughty Chil-
do) she told them, *That was the*
and that they ought to remember
keep it holy: And then she told
: was to be spent in religious Ex-
: Day long, except so much as
en up in the Works of Necessity
then she prayed with them her

self, and among other Things begged, *that the Lord would give Grace, and Wisdom to them little Children, that they might know how to serve him*; as one of the little Ones in the Company with her, told afterwards.

11. She was a Child of a strange Tenderness and Compassion to all, full of Bowels and Pity: Whom she could not help, she would weep over; especially if she saw her Mother at any Time troubled, she would quickly make her Sorrows her own, and weep for her, and with her.

12. When her Mother had been somewhat solicitous about any worldly Thing, she would, if she could, put her off from her Care one Way or other. One Time she told her, *O Mother, Grace is better than that*, (meaning something her Mother wanted,) *I had rather have Grace and the Love of Christ, than any Thing in the World.*

13. This Child was often musing and busied in the Thoughts of her everlasting Work; witness that strange Question, *O what are they doing, who are already in Heaven?* And she seem'd to be greatly desirous to be among 'em who were praising, loving, delighting in God, and serving of Him without Sin. Her Language was so strange about spiritual Matters, that she made many excellent Christians to stand amazed, as judging it scarce to be parallel'd.

14. She took great Delight in reading of

the Scripture, and some Part of it was more sweet to her than her appointed Food: She would get several choice Scriptures by Heart, and discourse of them savourly, and apply them suitably.

15. She was not altogether a stranger to other good Books, but would be reading of them with much Affection: and where she might, she noted the Books particularly, observing what in the reading did most warm her Heart, and she was ready upon Occasion to improve it.

16. One Time a Woman coming into the House in a great Passion, spoke of her Condition, as if none were like hers, and it would never be otherwise; the Child said, *It were a strange Thing to say when it is Night, it will never be Day again.*

17. At another Time a near Relation of her's being in some Streights made some Complaint; to whom she said, *I have heard Mr.* Carter *say, a Man may go to Heaven without a Penny in his Purse, but not without Grace in his Heart.*

18. She had an extraordinary Love to the People of God, and when she saw any that she tho't feared the Lord, her Heart would even leap for Joy.

19. She loved to be much by her self, and would be greatly grieved if she were at any Time deprived of a Conveniency for secret

C

Duty; she could not live without constant Address to God in secret; and was not a little pleased when she could go into a Corner to pray and weep.

20. She was much in praising God, and seldom or never complained of any thing but Sin.

21. She continued in this Course of praying and praising of God, and great Dutifulness and Sweetness to her Parents, and those that taught her any Thing, yet she did greatly encourage her Mother while she was a Widow, and desired, the Absence of a Husband, might in some Measure be made up by the Dutifulness and Holiness of a Child. She studied all the ways that could be to make her Mother's Life sweet.

22. When she was between eleven and twelve Years old, she sickned; in which she carried it with admirable Patience and Sweetness, and did what she could with Scripture Arguments, to support and encourage her Relations to part with her, who was going to Glory, and to prepare themselves to meet her in a blessed Eternity.

23. She was not many Days sick before she was marked; which she first saw her self, and was greatly rejoiced to think that she was marked out for the Lord, and was now going apace to Christ. She called to her Friends, and said, *I am marked, but be not troubled, for I know I am marked for one of the Lord's own.*

One asked her, *How she knew that?* She answered, *The Lord hath told me, that I am one of his dear Children.* And thus she spake with a holy Confidence in the Lord's Love to her Soul, and was not in the least daunted when she spake of her Death; but seemed greatly delighted in the Apprehension of her nearness to her Father's House: And it was not long before she was fill'd with Joy unspeakable in believing.

24. When she just lay a dying, her Mother came to her, and told her, *She was sorry that she had reproved and corrected so good a Child so oft.* O Mother, said she, *Speak not thus, I bless God, now I am dying, for your Reproofs and Corrections too; for it may be, I might have gone to Hell, if it had not been for your Reproofs and Corrections.*

25. Some of her Neighbours coming to visit her, asked her, *If she would leave them?* She answered them, *If you serve the Lord, you shall come after me to Glory.*

26. A little before she died, she had a great Conflict with Satan, and cried out, *I am none of his.* Her Mother seeing her in Trouble, asked her what was the Matter? She answered, *Satan did trouble me, but now I thank God all is well; I know I am not his, but Christ's.*

27. After this, she had a great Sense of God's Love, and a glorious Sight, as if she had seen the very Heavens open'd, and the Angels come to receive her; by which her

Heart was fill'd with Joy, and her Tongue with Praise.

28. Being desired by the standers by, to give them a particular Account of what she saw: she answer'd, *You shall know hereafter:* and so in an extasy of Joy and holy Triumph, she went to Heaven when she was about twelve Years old. *HALLELUJAH.*

EXAMPLE IV.

Of a Child that began to look towards Heaven when she was about Four Years old, with some observable Passages in her Life, and at her Death.

1. A Certain little Child, when she was about four Years old, had a consciencious Sense of her Duty towards her Parents, because the Commandment saith, *Honour thy Father and thy Mother.* And tho' she had little Advantage of Education, she carried it with the greatest Reverence to her Parents imaginable, so that she was no small Credit, as well as Comfort to them.

2. It was no unusual Thing for her to weep, if she saw her Parents troubled, tho' her self had not been the Occasion of it.

3. When she came from School, she would with Grief and Abhorrency say, *That other Children had sinned against God by speaking grievous Words, which were so bad, that she durst not speak them again.*

4. She would be often times admiring of God's Mercy, for so much Goodness to her rather than to others; that she saw some begging, others blind, some crooked, and that she wanted nothing that was good for her.

5. She was many a Time, and often, in one Hole or another, in Tears upon her Knees.

6. This poor little Thing would be ready to Counsel other little Children, how they ought to serve God; and putting them upon getting by themselves to pray; and hath been known when her Friends have been Abroad, to have been teaching Children to pray, especially upon the Lord's Day.

7. She very seriously begged the Prayers of others, that they would remember her, that the Lord would give her Grace.

8. When this Child saw some that were Laughing, who she judged to be very Wicked; she told them, *She feared they had little Reason to be merry.* They asked, *Whether one might not laugh?* She answered; *No indeed, 'till you have Grace! They who are Wicked, have more need to cry than to laugh.*

9. She would say, *That it was the Duty of Parents, Masters and Mistresses, to reprove (those under their Charge) for Sin, or else God will meet with them.*

10. She would be very attentive when she read the Scriptures, and be much affected with them.

11. She would by no Means be perswaded

C. 2

to profane the Lord's Day, but would spend it in some good Duties.

12. When she went to School, it was willingly and joyfully; and she was very teachable and exemplary to other Children.

13. When she was taken sick, one asked *Whether she were willing to die?* She answered, *Yes, if God would pardon her Sins.* Being asked, *How her Sins should be pardoned?* she answered, *Thro' the Blood of Christ.*

14. She said, *she did believe in Christ, and desired and longed to be with Him*; and did with a great deal of Chearfulness give up her Soul.

There were very many observable Passages, in the Life and Death of this Child, but the Hurry and Grief that her Friends were in, buried them.

EXAMPLE V.

Of the pious Life and joyful Death of a Child who died when he was about Twelve Years old, 1632.

1. CHarles Bridgman had no sooner learnt to speak, but he betook himself to Prayer.

2. He was very prone to learn the Things of God.

3. He would be sometimes teaching them their Duty, that waited upon him.

4. He learned by Heart many good things, before he was well fit to go to School (And

when he was sent to School, he carried it so, that all who observed him, either did or might admire him. O the sweet Nature, the good Disposition, the sincere Religion, which was in this Child!

5. When he was at School, what was it that he desired to learn, but Christ, and Him crucified?

6. So religious and savoury were his Words, his Actions so upright, his Devotion so hearty, his fear of God so great, that many were ready to say, as they did of *John*; *What Manner of Child shall this be?*

7. He would be much in reading the holy Scriptures.

8. He was desirous of more spiritual Knowledge, and would be often asking very serious and admirable Questions.

9. He would not stir out of Doors before he had poured out his Soul to the Lord.

10. When he eat any Thing, he would be sure to lift up his Heart unto the Lord for a Blessing upon it; and when he had moderately refreshed himself by eating, he would not forget to acknowledge God's Goodness in feeding of him.

11. He would not lie down in his Bed, 'till he had been upon his Knees; and when sometimes he had forgotten his Duty, he would quickly rise out of his Bed, and kneeling down upon his bare Knees; covered with no Gar-

ment but his Linnings, ask God forgiveness for that Sin.

12. He would rebuke his Brethren if they were at any Time too hasty at their Meals, and did eat without asking a Blessing; his Check was usually thus; *Dare you do thus? God be merciful to us, this Bit of Bread might choak us.*

13. His Sentences were wise and weighty, and well might become some ancient Christian.

14. His Sickness was a lingring Disease, against which to comfort him, one tells him of Possessions that must fall to his Portion: *And what are they,* said he, *I had rather have the Kingdom of Heaven, than a thousand such Inheritances.*

15. When he was sick, he seemed much taken up with Heaven, and asked very serious Questions about the Nature of his Soul.

16. After he was pretty well satisfied about that, *He enquired how his Soul might be saved?* The Answer being made; *by the applying of Christ's Merits by Faith*; he was pleased with the Answer, and was ready to give any one that should desire it, an Account of his Hope.

17. Being asked, whether he had rather live or die? He answered, *I desire to die, that I may go to my Saviour.*

18. His Pains encreasing upon him, one ask'd him, *Whether he would rather still endure those Pains, or forsake Christ?* Alas, said he, *I know not what to say, being but a Child: for*

these Pains may stagger a strong Man; but I will strive to endure the best that I can. Upon this he called to Mind that Martyr *Thomas Bilney*; who being in Prison, the Night before his burning, put his Finger into the Candle, to know how he could endure the Fire. O (said the Child) *had I lived then, I would have run through the Fire to have gone to Christ.*

19. His Sickness lasted long, and at least three Days before his Death, he prophesied his Departure, and not only that he must die, but the very Day. *On the Lord's Day,* said he, *look to me;* neither was this a Word of Course, which you may guess by his often Repetition, every Day asking 'till the Day came indeed, *What, is Sunday come?* At last, the look'd for Day came indeed, and no sooner had the Sun beautified that Morning with it's Light, but he falls into a Trance; his Eyes were fixed, his Face chearful, his Lips smiling, Hands and Feet clasped in a Bow, as if he would have received some blessed Angel that were at Hand to receive his Soul. But he comes to himself and tells them how he saw the sweetest Body that ever Eyes beheld, who bid him be of good Cheer, for he must presently go with him.

20. One that stood near him, as now suspecting the Time of his Dissolution nigh, bid him say, *Lord, into thy Hands I commend my Spirit, which is thy due; for why, thou hast redeemed it, O Lord, my God most true.*

21. The last Words which he spake, were exactly these: *Pray, pray, pray, nay, yet pray and the more Prayers, the better all prospers God is the best Physician*; *into his Hands I commend my Spirit. O Lord Jesus receive my Soul Now close mine Eyes: Forgive me, Father, Mother, Brother, Sister, all the World. Now I am well, my Pain is almost gone, my Joy is at Hand Lord have Mercy on me. O Lord receive my Soul unto thee.* And thus he yielded his Spirit up unto the Lord when he was about Twelve Years old.

This Narrative was taken out of Mr. Ambrose's *Life's Lease.*

EXAMPLE VI.

Of a poor Child that was awakened when he was about five Years old.

1. A Certain very poor Child that had a very bad Father, but it was to be hoped a very good Mother, was by the Providence of God, brought to the Sight of a godly Friend of mine, who upon the first Sight of the Child, had a great Pity for him, and took an Affection to him, and had a Mind to bring him up for Christ.

2. At the first, he did with great Sweetness and Kindness allure the Child; by which Means it was not long before he got a deep Interest in the Heart of the Child, and he be

him with more readiness than
lly do their Parents.
a Door was opened for a farther
he had a greater Advantage to
l Principles into the Soul of the
he was not wanting in, as the
Opportunity, and the Child was

not long before the Lord was
ike in with the spiritual Exhor-
s good Man, so that the Child
to a liking of the Things of God.
ickly learnt a great Part of the
atechism by Heart, and that be-
read his Primer within Book;
a great Delight in learning his

s not only able to give a very
it of his Catechism, but he would
Questions, as are not in the Cate-
reater Understanding than could
of one of his Age.
ok great Delight in discoursing
ings of God; and when my Friend
er praying or reading, expound-
ing of Sermons, he seemed very
l ready to receive the Truths of
uld with incredible Gravity, Di-
Affection, wait 'till Duties were
e no small Joy and Admiration
h observed him.
ild ask very excellent Questions,

and discourse about the Condition of his Soul and heavenly Things, and seemed mightily concerned what should become of his Soul when he should die: So that his Discourse made some Christians even to stand astonished.

9. He was greatly taken with the great Kindness of Christ in dying for Sinners, and would be in Tears at the mention of them: and seemed at a strange Rate to be affected with the unspeakable Love of Christ.

10. When no Body had been speaking to him, he would burst out into Tears, and being asked the Reason, he would say, *That the very Thoughts of Christ's Love to Sinners in suffering for them, made him that he could not but cry.*

11. Before he was six Years old, he made Conscience of secret Duty; and when he prayed, it was with such extraordinary Meltings, that his Eyes have looked red and sore, with weeping by himself for his Sin.

12. He would be putting of Christians upon spiritual Discourse when he saw them, and seemed little satisfied, unless they were talking of good Things.

13. It is evident, that this poor Child's Thoughts were very much busied about the Things of another World, for he would often times be speaking of his Bed-fellow at midnight about the Matters of his Soul; and when he could not sleep, he would take heavenly Conference to be sweeter than his ap-

pointed reſt. This was his uſual Cuſtom, and thus he would provoke and put forward an experienced Chriſtian, to ſpend waking Hours in talk of God and the everlaſting Reſt.

14. Not long after this, his good Mother died, which went very near his Heart, for he greatly honoured his Mother.

15. After the Death of his Mother, he would often repeat ſome of the Promiſes that are made to fatherleſs Children, eſpecially that in Exod. 22. 22. *Ye ſhall not afflict any Widow, or the fatherleſs Child, if thou afflict them in any wiſe, and they cry at all unto me, I will ſurely hear their Cry.*----Theſe Words he would often repeat with Tears, and ſay; *I am Fatherleſs and Motherleſs upon Earth, yet if any wrong me, I have a Father in Heaven who will take my Part; to Him I commit my ſelf, and in Him is all my Truſt.*

16. Thus he continued in a Courſe of holy Duties, living in the fear of God, and ſhewed wonderful Grace for a Child; and died ſweetly in the Faith of Jeſus.

My Friend, is a judicious Chriſtian of many Years Experience, who was no Ways related to him, but a conſtant and Ear-witneſs of his godly Life, and honourable and chearful Death, from whom I received this Information.

EXAMPLE VII.

Of a notorious wicked Child, who was taken up from begging, and admirably converted: with an Account of his holy Life and joyful Death, when he was nine Years old.

1. A Very poor Child, of the Parish of *Newington-Butts*, came begging to the Door of a dear Christian Friend of mine, in a very lamentable Case, so filthy and nasty, that he would have even turned one's Stomach to have looked on him: But it pleased God to raise in the Heart of my Friend, a great Pity and Tenderness towards this poor Child, so that in Charity he took him out of the Streets, whose Parents were unknown; and who had nothing at all to commend him to any one's Charity, but his Misery. My Friend eying the Glory of God, and the Good of the immortal Soul of this wretched Creature, discharged the Parish of the Child, and took him as his own, designing to bring him up for the Lord Christ. A noble Piece of Charity! And that which did make the Kindness far the greater, was that there seemed to be very little Hopes of doing any Good upon this Child, for he was a very Monster of Wickedness, and a thousand Times more miserable and vile by his Sin, than by his Poverty. He was running to Hell as soon as he could go, and was old in Naughtiness when he was young

in Years; and One shall scarce hear of a Person so like the Devil in his Infancy, as this poor Child was. What Sin was there (that his Age was capable of) that he did not commit? What by the Corruption of his Nature, and the abominable Example of little beggar Boys, he was arrived to a strange Pitch of impiety. He would call filthy Names, take God's Name in vain, Curse and Swear, and do almost all Kind of Mischief; and as to any Thing of God, worse than an Heathen.

2. But this Sin and Misery was but a stronger Motive to that gracious Man to pity him, and to do all that possibly he could to pluck this Fire-brand out of the Fire; and it was not long before the Lord was pleased to let him understand, that he had a Design of everlasting Kindness upon the Soul of this poor Child; for no sooner had this good Man taken this Creature into his House, but he prays for him, and labours with all his might to convince him of his Miserable Condition by Nature, and to teach him something of God, the Worth of his own Soul, and that Eternity of Glory or Misery that he was born to: And blessed be free Grace, it was not long before the Lord was pleased to let him understand, that it was himself which put it into his Heart to take in this Child, that he might bring him up for Christ. The Lord soon struck in with his godly Instruction, so that an amazing change was seen in the Child; in a few Weeks

Time he was convinced of the Evil of his Ways; no more News now of his calling of Names, Swearing, or Cursing; no more taking of the Lord's Name in vain: now he is civil and respective, and such a strange Alteration was wrought in the Child, that all the Parish that rung of his Villany before, was now ready to talk of his Reformation; his Company, his Talk, his Employment is now changed, and he is like another Creature; so that the Glory of God's free Grace began already to shine in him.

3. And this Change was not only an external one, and to be discerned Abroad, but he would get by himself, and weep and mourn bitterly, for his horrible wicked Life, as might easily be perceived by them that lived in the House with him.

4. It was the great Care of his godly Master to strike in with those Convictions which the Lord had made, and to improve them all he could; and he was not a little glad to see his Labour was not in vain in the Lord: He still experiences that the Lord doth carry on his own Work mightily upon the Heart of the Child: He is still more and more broken under a Sense of his undone State by Nature: He is oft in Tears, and bemoaning his lost and miserable Condition. When his Master did speak of the things of God, he listened earnestly, and took in with much greediness and affection what he was taught. Seldom was

there any Discourse about Soul Matters in his Hearing, but he heard it as if it were for his Life, and would weep greatly.

5. He would after his Master had been speaking to him, or others, of the Things of God, go to him, and question with him about them, and beg of him to instruct and teach him further, and to tell him those things again, that he might remember and understand them better.

6. Thus he continued seeking after the Knowledge of God and Christ, and practising holy Duties, till the Sickness came into the House, with which the Child was smitten; at his first sickning, the poor Child was greatly amazed and afraid, and though his Pains were great, and the Distemper very tedious, yet the Sense of his Sin, and the Thought of the miserable Condition that he feared his Soul was still in, made his Trouble ten Times greater: He was in grievous Agonies of Spirit, and his former Sins stared him in the Face, and made him tremble; the Poison of God's Arrows did even drink up his Spirits; the Sense of Sin and Wrath was so great, that he could not tell what in the World to do; the Weight of God's Displeasure, and the Tho't of lying under it to all Eternity, did even break him to Pieces, and he did Cry out very bitterly, *What should he do? He was a miserable Sinner, and he feared that he should go to Hell*; his Sins

had been so great and so many, *that there was no Hopes for him.* He was not by far so much concerned for his Life, as for his Soul, what would become of that for ever. Now the Plague upon his Body seemed nothing to that which was in his Soul.

7. But in this great Distress the Lord was pleased to send One to take care for his Soul, who urged to him the great and precious Promises which were made to one in his Condition; telling him, *There was enough in Christ for the chiefest of Sinners*; and *that He came to seek and save such a lost Creature as he was.* But this poor Child found it a very difficult Thing for him to believe that there was any Mercy for such a dreadful Sinner as he had been.

8. He was made to cry out of himself, not only for his Swearing and Lying, and other outwardly notorious Sins; but he was in great Horror for the Sin of his Nature, for the Vileness of his Heart, and original Corruption; under it he was in so great Anguish, that the Trouble of his Spirit, made him in a great Measure to forget the Pains of his Body.

9. He did very particularly confess and bewail his Sins with Tears; and some Sins so secret, that none in the World could charge him with.

10. He would condemn himself for Sin, as deserving no Mercy; and tho't that there was not a greater Sinner in all *London* than him-

self, and he abhorred himself as the vilest Creature he knew.

11. He did not only pray much with strong Cries and Tears himself, but he begged the Prayers of Christians for him.

12. He would ask Christians, whether they tho't there were any Hopes for him, and would beg of them to deal plainly with him, for he was greatly afraid of being deceived.

13. Being inform'd how willing and ready the Lord Christ was to accept of poor Sinners, upon their Repentance and Turning, and being counselled to venture himself upon Christ for Mercy and Salvation, he said, *He would fain cast himself upon Christ, but he could not but wonder, how Christ should be willing to die for such a vile Wretch as he was;* and that *he found it one of the hardest Things in the World to believe.*

14. But at last it pleased the Lord to give him some small Hopes that there might be Mercy for him, for he had been the chiefest of Sinners; and was made to lay a little Hold upon such Promises, as that, *Come unto me, all ye that are weary and heavy laden, and I will give you rest.* But O! how did this *poor Boy* admire and bless God for the least *Hopes!* How highly did he advance free and rich Grace, that should Pity and Pardon him! And at last he was full of Praise, and admiring of God; so that (to speak in the Words of a precious Man, who was an Eye and Ear Witness)

to the Praise and Glory of God, be it spoken, the House at that Day, for all the Sickness in it, was a little lower Heaven, so full of Joy and Praise.

15. The Child grew exceedingly in *Knowledge*, *Experience*, *Patience*, *Humility* and *Self-abhorrency*; and he thought he could never speak bad enough of himself, the Name that he would call himself by, was a *Toad*.

16. And tho' he prayed before, yet now the Lord poured out upon him the Spirit of Prayer, in an extraordinary Manner for one of his Age; so that now he prayed more frequently, more earnestly, more spiritually than ever. O how eagerly would he beg to be washed in the Blood of Jesus! And that the *King of Kings*, and *Lord of Lords*, that was over Heaven and Earth, and Sea, would pardon and forgive him all his Sins, and receive his Soul into his Kingdom. And what he spoke, it was with so much Life and fervor of Spirit, as that it filled the Hearers with Astonishment and Joy.

17. He had no small Sense of the Use and Excellency of Christ, and such Longings and Breathings of his Soul after him, that when mention hath been made of *Christ*, he hath been ready almost to leap out of his Bed for Joy.

18. When he was told, *that if he should recover, he must not live as he list; but he must give up himself to Christ, and to be his Child and Servant, to bear his Yoke and be obedient to his Laws, and live a holy Life, and take his Cross,*

and suffer Mocking and Reproach, it may be, Persecution for his Names Sake. Now, Child, (said one to him) *are you willing to have Christ upon such Terms?* He signified his Willingness by the Earnestness of his Looks and Words, and the casting up of his Eyes to Heaven, saying, *Yes with all my Soul, the Lord helping me, I will do this.*

19. Yet he had many Doubts and Fears, and was ever and anon harping upon that, *That tho' he were willing, yet Christ he feared was not willing to accept him, because of the greatness of his Sins*; yet his Hopes were greater than his Fears.

20. The *Wednesday* before he died, the Child lay as it were in a Trance for about half an Hour, in which Time he thought he saw a Vision of Angels: When he was out of his Trance, he was in a little Pett, and asked his Nurse, *Why she did not let him go?* Go, whither Child, said she: *Why along with those brave Gentlemen* (said he) *but they told me they would come and fetch me for all of you upon* Friday *next.* And he doubled his Words many Times, *Upon* Friday *next, those brave Gentlemen will come for me*; and upon that Day, the Child died joyfully.

21. He was very thankful to his Master, and very sensible of his great Kindness in taking him out of the Streets, when he was a begging: and he admired at the Goodness of God, which put it into the Mind of a Stranger

to look upon, and to take such a f[...]
of such a pitiful sorry Creature as [...]
my dear Master, (said he) *and Ser*[...]
I hope to see you in Heaven, for I [...]
will go thither. O blessed, blessed [...]
made you to take Pity upon me, for [...]
died, and have gone to the Devil, a[...]
damned for ever, if it had not been f[...]

22. The *Thursday* before he di[...]
a very godly Friend of mine, *Wh*[...]
of his Condition, and whither his S[...]
going? For he said, *He could not j*[...]
least he should deceive himself with [...]
At which my Friend spoke to him [...]
For all that I have endeavoured to h[...]
Grace of God in Christ to thy Soul, a[...]
a Warrant from the Word of God, t[...]
as freely offered to you, as to any S[...]
World; if thou art but willing to a[...]
thou mayst have Christ, and all th[...]
want with Him; and yet thou dost [...]
these thy Doubtings and Fears, as i[...]
nothing but Lies. Thou sayest, thou [...]
Christ will not accept of thee; I f[...]
not heartily willing to accept of Him. [...]
answered, *Indeed I am:* Why the [...]
thou art unfeignedly willing to have [...]
thee, He is a thousand Times more wi[...]
thee, and wash thee, and save thee [...]
art to desire it. And now at this [...]
offers himself freely to thee again [...]
receive him humbly by Faith into [...]

and bid him welcome, for he deserveth it. Upon which Words the Lord discovered his Love to the Child, and he gave a Kind of a Leap in his Bed, and snapt his Fingers and Thumb together with Abundance of Joy, as much as to say, *Well, yea all is well, the Match is made, Christ is willing, and I am willing too; and now Christ is mine, and I am his for ever.* And from that Time forward, in full Joy and Assurance of God's Love, he continued earnestly praising God, with desiring to die, and be with Christ. And on *Friday Morning* he sweetly went to Rest, using that very Expression, *Into thy Hands, Lord, I commit my Spirit.* He died punctually at that Time which he had spoke of, and in which he expected those Angels to come to him; he was not much above nine Years old when he died.

This Narrative I had from a judicious holy Man, unrelated to him, who was an Eye and Ear-Witness to all these Things.

EXAMPLE VIII.

Of a Child that was very serious at four Years old, with an Account of his comfortable Death, when he was twelve Years and three Weeks old.

JOHN *Sudlow*, was born of religious Parents, in the County of *Middlesex*, whose great Care was to instill spiritual Principles into him, as soon as he was capable of understanding of them; whose Endeavours the Lord was pleased to Crown with the desired Success; So that (to use the Expression of a holy Man concerning him) *Scarce more could be expected or desired from so little a One.*

2. When he was scarce able to speak plain, he seemed to have a very great Awe and Reverence of God upon his Spirit, and a strange Sense of the Things of another World, as might easily be perceived by those serious and admirable Questions which he would be oft asking of those Christians that he thought he might be bold with.

3. The first Thing that did most affect him, and made him endeavour to escape from the Wrath to come, and to enquire what he should do to be saved, was the Death of a little Brother; when he saw him without Breath, and not able to speak or stir, and then carried out of Doors, and put into a Pit-hole, he was greatly concerned, and asked notable Questions about him; but that which was most affecting of himself and others, was, *Whether he must Die too?* which being answered, it made such a deep Impression upon him, that from that Time forward, he was exceeding serious, and this was when he was about four Years old.

4. Now he is desirous to know what he might do that he might live in another World, and what he must avoid, that he might not dye for ever, and being instructed by his god-

ly Parents, he foon labours to avoid whatfoever might difpleafe God; now tell him that any Thing was finful, and that God would not have him to do it, and he is eafily kept from it, and even at this Time of Day, the Apprehenfions of God and Death and Eternity laid fuch a Reftraint upon him, that he would not for a World have told a Lie.

5. He quickly learned to read exactly, and took fuch Pleafure in reading of the Scriptures and his Catechifm, and other good Books, that it is fcarce to be parallel'd; he would naturally run to his Book without bidding, when he came Home from School, and when other Children of his Age and Acquaintance were playing, he reckon'd it his Recreation to be doing that which is good.

6. When he was in Coats, he would be ftill afking his Maid ferious Queftions, and praying her to teach him his Catechifm, or Scriptures, or fome good thing; common-Difcourfe he took no delight in, but did moft eagerly defire to be fucking in of the knowledge of the Things of God, Chrift, his Soul, and another World.

7. He was hugely taken with the reading of the Book of *Martyrs*, and would be ready to leave his Dinner to go to his Book.

8. He was exceeding careful of redeeming and improving of Time; fcarce a Moment of it, but he would give an excellent Account of

E

the Expence of it; so that this Child might have taught elder Persons, and will questionless condemn their idle and unaccountable wasting of those precious Hours in which they should (as this sweet Child,) have been laying in Provision for Eternity.

9. He could not endure to read any Thing over slightly, but whatsoever he read, he dwelt upon it, laboured to understand it throughly, and remember it, and what he could not understand, he would oft ask his Father or Mother the Meaning of it.

10. When any Christian Friends have been discoursing with his Father, if they began to talk any Thing about Religion, to be sure they should have his Company, and of his own Accord, he would leave all to hear any Thing of Christ, and crept as close to them as he could, and listen as affectionately, though it were for an Hour or two: He was scarce ever known to express the least Token of Weariness while he was hearing any Thing that was Good, and sometimes, when Neighbours Children would come and call him out, and entice him, and beg of him to go with them, he could by no Means be perswaded, (though he might have had the Leave of his Parents,) if he had any Hopes that any good Body would come into his Father's House.

11. He was very modest while any Stranger was present, and was loth to ask them any Questions: but as soon as they were gone, he

would let his Father know that there was little said or done, but he obferved it, and would reflect upon what was paft in their Difcourfe, and defire Satisfaction in what he could not underftand at prefent.

12. He was a Boy of moft prodigious Parts for his Age, as will appear from his folid and rational Queftions; I fhall mention but two of many..

13. The firft was this, when he was reading by himfelf, in *Draiton*'s Poems about *Noah*'s Flood and the Ark, he afked, *Who built the Ark?* It being anfwered, that it was likely that *Noah* hired Men to help him build it: *And would they* (faid he) *build an Ark to fave another, and not go into it themfelves?*

14. Another Queftion he put was this: *Whether had a greater Glory, Saints or Angels?* It being anfwered, that Angels were the moft excellent of Creatures, and it's to be thought, their Nature is made capable of greater Glory than Man's. He faid, *He was of another Mind, and his Reafon was, becaufe Angels were Servants, and Saints are Children; and that Chrift never took upon him the Nature of Angels, but he took upon him the Nature of Saints, and by his being* MAN, *He hath advanced humane Nature above the Nature of Angels.*

15. By this you may perceive the greatnefs of his Parts, and the bent of his Thoughts; and thus he continued for feveral Years together, labouring to get more and more fpiritual

Knowledge, and to prepare for an endless Life.

16. He was a Child of an excellent sweet Temper, wonderfully dutiful to his Parents, ready and joyful to do what he was bid, and by no Means would do any Thing to displease them, and if they were at any Time seemingly Angry, he would not stir from them, till they were thoroughly reconciled to him.

17. He was not only good himself, but would do what he could to make others so too, especially those that were nearest to him; he was very watchful over his Brethren and Sisters, and would not suffer them to use any unhandsome Words, or to do any unhandsome Action, but he would be putting them upon that which was Good; and when he did at any Time rebuke them, it was not childishly and slightly, but with great Gravity, and Seriousness, as one that was not a little concerned for God's Honour, and the eternal Welfare of their Souls.

18. He would go to his Father and Mother with great Tenderness and Compassion, (being far from telling of Tales) and beg of them, to take more Care of the Souls of his Brethren and Sisters; and to take heed, lest they should go on in a sinful Christless State, and prove their Sorrow and Shame, and go to Hell when they die, and be ruined forever.

19. He was exceedingly affected with hearing of the Word of God preached, and could not be satisfied, except he could carry home

much of the Substance of what he heard; to this end he quickly got to learn short Hand, and would give a very pretty Account of any Sermon that he heard.

20. He was much engaged in secret Duty, and in reading the Scriptures; to be sure Morning and Evening he would be by himself, and was no Question, wrestling with God.

21. He would get choice Scriptures by Heart, and was very perfect at his Catechism.

22. The Providences of God were not passed by, without considerable Observation by him.

23. In the Time of the Plague, he was exceedingly concerned about his Soul and everlasting State; and much by himself upon his Knees. This Prayer was found written in Short-Hand after his Death.

O Lord God and merciful Father, take Pity upon me a miserable Sinner, and strengthen me, O Lord, in thy Faith, and make me one of thy glorious Saints in Heaven. O Lord, keep me from this poisonous Infection; however, not my Will but thy Will be done, O Lord, on Earth, as it is in Heaven; but, O Lord, if thou hast appointed me to die by it, O Lord, fit me for Death, and give me a good Heart to bear up under my Afflictions: O Lord God and merciful Father, take Pity on me thy Child; teach me O Lord thy Word, make me strong in Faith. O Lord, I have sinned against thee; Lord pardon my Sins. I had been in Hell long ago if it had not been for thy Mercy: O Lord, I pray thee to keep my Parents in thy Truth, and save them from this Infection, if it be thy Will, that they may live to bring me up in thy Truth: O Lord I pray thee stay this Infection that rageth in this City, and pardon their Sins, and try them once more, and see if they will turn unto thee. Save me, O Lord, from this Infection, that I may live to praise and glorify thy Name; but, O Lord, if thou hast appointed me to die of it, fit me for Death, that I may die with Comfort; and, O Lord, I pray thee to help me to bear up under all Afflictions; for Christ's Sake. Amen.

24. He was not a little concerned for the whole Nation, and begged that God would pardon the Sins of this Land, and bring it nearer to himself.

25. About the beginning of *November* 1665, this sweet Child was smote with the Distemper, but he carried it with admirable Patience under the Hand of God.

26. These are some of his dying Expressions---*The Lord shall be my Physician, for he will cure both Soul and Body.*---*Heaven is the best Hospital:*---*It is the Lord, let him do what seemeth Good in his Eyes.*---Again,---*It is the Lord that taketh away my Health; but I will say as* Job *said,* Blessed be the Name of the Lord.---*If I should live longer, I shall but sin against God.* Looking upon his Father, he said, *If the Lord would but lend me the least*

Finger of his Hand, to lead me thro' the dark Entry of Death, I will rejoyce in him.

27. When a Minister came to him, among other Things, he spake somewhat of Life. He said, *This is a wicked World, yet it is good to live with my Parents, but it is better to live in Heaven.*

28. An Hour and a half before his Death, the same Minister came again to visit him, and asked him, *John, Art thou afraid to die ?* He answered; *No, If the Lord will but comfort me in that Hour.* But said the Minister, *How canst thou expect Comfort, seeing we deserve none ?* He answered, *No, if I had my Deserts, I had been in Hell long ago.* But replied the Minister, *Which Way dost thou expect Comfort and Salvation, seeing thou art a Sinner.* He answered, *In Christ alone.*---In whom about an Hour and an half after, he fell asleep, saying, *He would take a long Sleep, Charging them that were about him not to wake him.*

He died when he was twelve Years three Weeks and one Day old.

EXAMPLE IX.

Of a Child that was very eminent, when she was between Five and Six Years old, with some memorable Passages of her Life, who died about 1640.

1. A*Nne Lane* was born of honest Parents in *Colebrook*, in the County of *Bucks*,

who was no sooner able to speak plain, and express any Thing considerable of Reason, but she began to act as if she were sanctified from the very Womb.

2. She was very solicitous about her Soul, what would become of it when she should die, and where she should live for ever, and what she should do to be saved, when she was about Five Years old.

3. She was wont to be oft engaged in secret Prayer, and pouring out her Soul in such a Manner, as is rarely to be heard of from one of her Years.

4. I having Occasion to lie at *Colebrook*, sent for her Father, an old Disciple, an *Israelite* indeed, and desired him to give me some Account of his Experiences, and how the Lord first wrought upon him?

5. He gave me this answer, " That he was
" of a Child somewhat civil ; honest, and as
" to a Man, harmless ; but he was little ac-
" quainted with the Power of Religion, 'till
" this sweet Child put him upon a thorow In-
" quiry into the State of his Soul, and would
" still be begging of him, and pleading with
" him to redeem his Time, and to act with
" Life and Vigour in the Things of God,
" which was no small Demonstration to him
" of the Reality of Invisibles, that a very Babe
" and Suckling should speak so feelingly a-
" bout the Things of God, and be so greatly
" concerned, not only about her own Soul,

" but about her Father's too, which was the
" Occasion of his Conversion, and the very
" Thought of it was a quickening to him for
" thirty Years, and he hopes never to wear
" off the Impression of it from his Spirit.

6. After this she (as I remember) put her Father upon Family Duties, and if he were for any Time out of his Shop, she would find him out, and with much Sweetness and Humility beg of him to come Home, and to remember the Preciousness of Time, for which we must all give an Account.

7. She was grieved if she saw any that conversed with her Father if they were unprofitable, unsavory, or long in their Discourse of common Things.

8. Her own Language was the Language of *Canaan*: How solidly, profitably, and spiritually would she talk? So that she made good People take great Delight in her Company, and justly drew the Admiration of all that knew her.

9. She could not endure the Company of common Children, nor Play, but was quite above all those Things which most Children are taken with; her Business was to be reading, praying, discoursing about the Things of God, and any Kind of Business that her Age and Strength was capable of; idle she would not be by any Means.

10. It was the greatest Recreation to her to hear any good People talking about God,

Chrift, their Souls, the Scriptu
Thing that concerned another Li

11. She had a ftrange Cont
World, and fcorned thofe Thing
are too much pleafed with. She
brought to wear any Laces, or an
fhe thought fuperfluous.

12. She would be complainin
rents if fhe faw any Thing in tl
judged would not be for the Hc
ligion, or fuitable to that Conditi
Providence of God had fet thei
World.

13. This Child was the Joy an
all the Chriftians there-abouts, in
who was ftill quickning and ra
Spirits of thofe that talked with
poor Babe was a great Help to
and Mother, and her Memory is
Day.

14. She continued thus to
Stranger in the World, and one th
ing hafte to a better Place. A
had done a great Deal of Work f
her own Soul, and others too, fh
Home to reft, and received into
JESUS, before fhe was ten Yea
departed obout 1640.

Of a Child that was awakened when she was between Seven and Eight Years old, with some Account of her last Hours, and triumphant Death.

1. Tabitha Alder was a Daughter of a holy and reverend Minister in *Kent*, who lived near *Gravesend*. She was much instructed in the holy Scriptures and her Catechism, by her Father and Mother, but there appeared nothing extraordinary in her, till she was between Seven and Eight Years old.

2. About which Time, when she was sick, one asked her, *What she thought would become of her if she should die?* She answered, *That she was greatly afraid she should go to Hell.*

3. Being asked, *Why she was afraid of going to Hell?* She answered, *Because she feared she did not love God.*

4. Again, being asked, *How she did know that she did not love God?* She replied, *What have I done for God ever since I was born? And besides this, I have been taught, That he that loves God keeps his Commandments, but I have kept none of them all.*

5. Being further demanded, *If she would not fain love God?* She answered, *Yes, with all her Heart, if she could, but she found it a hard Thing to love one she did not see.*

6. She was advised to beg of God a Heart

to love him: she answered, *She a*
was too late.

7. Being asked again, *whether
sorry that she could not love God?* S
Yes, but was still afraid it was too

8. Upon this, seeing her in suc
ing Condition, a dear Friend of h
next Day in Fasting and Prayer f

9. After this, that Christian l
her how she did now? She ans
great Deal of Joy, that now sh
Lord, she loved the Lord Jesu
felt she did love him, *Oh, said sh
dearly.*

10. Why said her Friend, did
Yesterday, that you did not lov
and that you could not? What d
to speak so strangely? *Sure* (sai
*Satan that did put it into my Min
I love him, O blessed be God for th
Christ.*

11. After this, she had a disc
approaching Dissolution, which
comfort to her: *Anon* (said she,
Triumph) *I shall be with Jesus, .
to him, he is my Husband, I am his
given my self to him, and he hath
to me, and I sh*[a]*ll live with him fo*

12. This strange Language ma
ers even stand astonished: But t
tinued for some little Time, in a
tasy of Joy, admiring the Excellen

rejoicing in her Interest in him, and longing to be with Him.

13. After a while, some of her Friends standing by her, observed a more than ordinary Earnestness and Fixedness in her Countenance; they said one to another, Look how earnestly she looks, sure she seeth something.

14. One asked, What it was she fixed her Eyes upon so eagerly; I warrant (saith one that was by) she seeth Death a coming.

15. No, (said she,) *it is Glory that I see, 'tis that I fix my Eye upon.*

16. One ask'd her, What was Glory like? She answered, *I can't speak what, but I am going to it; will you go with me? I am going to Glory, O that all you were to go with me to that Glory?* With which Words her Soul took Wing, and went to the Possession of that Glory which she had some believing Sight of before.

She died when she was between eight and nine Years old, about 1644.

EXAMPLE XI.

Of a Child that was greatly affected with the Things of God, when she was very Young, with an exact Account of her admirable Carriage upon her Death Bed.

1. SUsannah Bicks was born at *Leiden* in *Holland*, *Jan.* 24. 1650, of very reli-

gious Parents, whose great Care was to instruct and catechise this their Child, and to present her to the Ministers of the Place, to be publickly instructed and catechised.

2. It pleased the Lord to bless the holy Education, and good Example of her Parents, and Catechising, to the good of her Soul, so that she soon had a true Savour and Relish of what she was taught, and made an admirable Use of it in a Time of Need, as you shall hear afterwards.

3. She was a Child of great Dutifulness to her Parents, and of a sweet, humble, spiritual Nature, and not only the Truth, but the Power and Eminency of Religion did shine in her so clearly, that she did not only comfort the Hearts of her Parents, but drew the Admiration of all that were Witnesses of God's Works of Love upon her, and may well be proposed as a Pattern not only to Children, but to Persons of riper Years.

4. She continued in a Course of religious Duties for some considerable Time, so that her Life was more excellent than most Christians, but in her last Sickness she excelled herself, and her Deportment was so admirable, that partly thro' Wonder and Astonishment, and partly thro' Sorrow, many observable Things were pass'd by without committing to Paper, which deserved to have been written in Letters of Gold: But take these which follow, as some of the many which were taken

from her dying Lips, and first published by religious and judicious Christians in *Dutch*, afterward translated into *Scotch*, and with a little Alteration of the Stile, (for the Benefit of *English* Children) brought into this Form by me.

5. In the Month of *August*, 1664, when the Pestilence raged so much in *Holland*, this sweet Child was smitten, and as soon as she felt her self very ill, she was said to break forth with abundance of Sense and Feeling, in these following Words ; *If thy Law were not my Delight, I should perish in my Affliction.*

6. Her Father coming to her to encourage her in her sickness, said to her, *Be of good Comfort my Child, for the Lord will be near to thee and us, under the heavy Trial ; He will not forsake us tho' he chasten us.* Yea Father (said she) *our heavenly Father doth chasten us for our Profit, that we may be Partakers of his Holiness: No Chastisement seemeth for the present to be joyous but grievous, yet afterwards it yieldeth the peaceable Fruits of Righteousness to them which are exercised thereby. The Lord is now chastening of me upon this sick Bed, but I hope he will bless it so to me, as to cause it to yield to me that blessed Fruit, according to the Riches of his Mercies, which fail not.*

7. After this, she spake to God with her Eyes lift up to Heaven, saying, *Be merciful to me, O Father, be merciful to me a Sinner, according to thy Word.*

8. Then, looking upon her fo[rmer?] rents, she said, It is said, *Cast thy [Burden on?] the Lord, and He shall sustain thee, [and will?] never suffer the Righteous to be mov[ed]:* [There]fore, my dear Father and Mother, [cast your?] *Care upon Him, who causes all Thin[gs]* that do concern you.

9. Her Mother said unto her, [Dear] Child, I have no small Comfort from thee, and the Fruit of his Grace, [that thou] hast been so much exercised unto Godl[iness, seek]ing the Word, in Prayer and gracio[us Conference] to the Edification of thy self and us. [God] Himself who gave thee to us, make [us content] if it be his Pleasure to take thee aw[ay].

10. *Dear Mother,* (said she) *tho' [I part with] and you me, yet God will never leave [us. It] is said, Can a Woman forget her Su[ckling,] that she should not have Compassion [on the Son] of her Womb, yet will not I forget th[ee.] I have graven thee upon the Palms [of my Hands.] O comfortable Words, both for Mot[hers and Chil]dren! Mark, dear Mother, How [faithfully God] keeps and holdeth his People, that [he hath] grave them upon the Palms of his H[ands].* I must part with you, and you with [me, bles]sed be God, He will never part eit[her with you] or me.

11. Being weary with much s[peaking, she] desired to rest awhile; but after a [little, and] awaking again, her Father asked, [how it was] with her? She made no direct A[nswer,]

asked what Day it was? Her Father said, It was the Lord's Day? Well then, said she, Have you given up my Name to be remembred in the publick Prayers of the Church? Her Father told her he had. I have learnt, said she, *That the effectual fervent Prayer of the Righteous availeth much.*

12. She had a very high Esteem for the faithful Ministers of Christ, and much desired their Company where she was, but knowing the Hazard that such a Visit might expose them and the Church to, she would by no Means suffer that the Ministers should come near her Person, but chose rather to throw herself upon the Arms of the Lord, and to improve that Knowledge she had in the Word, and her former Experience, and the Visits of private Christians, and those which the Church had appointed in such Cases, to visit and comfort the Sick.

13. One of those which came to visit her, was of very great Use to comfort her, and lift her up in some Measure above the Fears of Death.

14. Tho' Young, she was very much concerned for the Interest of God and Religion, for Gospel-Ministers, and for the Sins and the Decay of the Power of Godliness in her own Country, which will further appear, by what may follow.

15. Her Father coming in to her, found

her in an extraordinary Paſſion of Weeping, and aſked her what was the Cauſe of her great Sorrow: She anſwered, Have I not cauſe to weep, when I hear that *Domine de Wit* was taken ſick this Day in his Pulpit, and went Home very Ill? Is not this a ſad Sign of God's Diſpleaſure to our Country, when God ſmiteth ſuch a faithful Paſtor.

16. She had a high Valuation of God, and could ſpeak in *David*'s Language, *Whom have I in Heaven but Thee, and there is none on Earth that I can deſire in Compariſon of Thee.* She was much lifted above the Fears of Death; what elſe was the Meaning of ſuch Expreſſions as theſe? *O how do I long! even as the Heart panteth after thee, O God, for God, the living God, when ſhall I come and appear before God.*

17. She was a great hater of Sin, and did with much Grief and Self-Abhorrency reflect upon it; but that which lay moſt upon her Heart, was the Corruption of her Nature and original Sin. How oft would ſhe cry out in the Words of the Pſalmiſt, *Behold, I was ſhapen in Iniquity, and in Sin did my Mother conceive me: And I was altogether born in Sin.* She could never lay her ſelf low enough under a Senſe of that original Sin which ſhe brought with her into the World.

18. She ſpake many Things very judiciouſly of the old Man, and putting it off, and of the new Man, and putting that on; which

shewed that she was no Stranger to Conversion, and that she in some Measure understood what Mortification, Self-denial, and taking up of her Cross, and fo'lowing Christ, meant. That Scripture was much in her Mouth, *The Sacrifices of God are a contrite Heart; a broken and a contrite Spirit, O God, thou wilt not despise.* That Brokenness of Heart (said she) *which is built upon, and flows from Faith, and that Faith which is built upon Christ, who is the proper and alone Sacrifice for Sin.* These are her own Words.

19. Afterwards she desired to rest, and when she had slumbered a while, she said, O dear Father and Mother, how weak do I feel my self! My dear Child! (said her Father) God will in his tender Mercy strengthen thee in thy Weakness. Yea Father, (said she) that is my Confidence: For it is said, *The bruised Reed he will not break, and the smoaking Flax he will not quench.*

20. Then she discoursed excellently of the Nature of Faith, and desired that the Eleventh of the *Hebrews* should be read unto her; at the reading of which she cried out, O, what a stedfast loyal Faith was that of *Abraham*, which made him willing to offer up his own and only Son! *Faith is the Substance of Things hoped for, and the Evidence of Things not seen.*

21. Her Father and Mother hearing her excellent Discourse, and seeing her admirable Carriage, burst out into Abundance of Tears:

Upon which she pleaded with them to be patient, and content with the Hand of God. O (said she) why do you weep at this Rate over me, seeing I hope, you have no Reason to Question, but if the Lord take me out of this miserable World, it shall be well with me to all Eternity. You ought to be well satisfied, seeing it is said, *God is in Heaven, and doth whatsoever pleaseth Him*: And do not you pray every Day, *That the Will of God may be done upon Earth, as it is in Heaven?* Now Father, This is God's Will that I should lie upon this sick Bed, and of this Disease; shall we not be content when our Prayers are answered? Would not your extream Sorrow be murmuring against God, without whose good Pleasure nothing comes to pass. Altho' I am struck with this sad Disease, yet because it is the Will of God, that doth silence me, and I will as long as I live, pray that God's Will may be done, and not mine.

22. Seeing her Parents still very much moved, she further argued with them from the Providence of God, which had a special Hand in every common Thing, much more in the disposal of the Lives of Men and Women: *Are not two Sparrows sold for a Farthing, and not one of them falls to the Ground without our heavenly Father?* Yea, *The Hairs of our Head are all numbred: therefore fear not, you are of more Value than many Sparrows.* Adversity and Prosperity they are both good. Some

Things appear Evil in our Eyes, but the Lord turns all to the Good of them which are his.

23. She came then to speak particularly concerning the Plague. Doth not (said she) the Pestilence come from God? Why elle doth the Scripture say, *Shall there be Evil in the City which I have not sent?* What do those People mean, which say, the Pestilence comes from the Air? Is not the Lord the Creator and Ruler of the Air, and are not the Elements under his Government? Or if they say, it comes from the Earth, hath he not the same Power and Influence upon that too? Why talk they of a Ship that came from *Africa*; have we not read long ago together, out of Lev. 26. 25. *I shall bring a Sword upon you, and evenge the Quarrel of my Covenant; and when you are assembled in the Cities, then will I bring the Pestilence in the midst of you.*

24. After this, having taken some little Rest, she said, O now is the Day for opening of the first Question of the Catechism, and if we were there, we should hear, that whether in Death or Life, a Believer is Christ's who hath redeemed us by his own precious Blood from the Power of the Devil: And then she quoted, Rom. 14. 7, 8. *For none of us liveth unto himself, and none of us dieth unto himself. For whether we live we live unto the Lord, and whether we die we die unto the Lord; whether then we live or die, we are the Lord's.* Then be comforted, for whether I live or die, I am

the Lord's. O why do you afflict yourselves thus! But what shall I say? With weeping I came into the World, and with weeping I must go out again. O my dear Parents, Better is the Day of my Death, than the Day of my Birth.

27. When she had thus encouraged her Father and Mother, she desired her Father to pray with her, and to request of the Lord that she might have a quiet and peaceable Passage into another World.

26. After her Father had prayed for her, he asked her, whether he should send for the Physician; she answered, By no Means, for I am now beyond the help of Doctors. But said he, my Child, we are to use the ordinary Means appointed by the Lord for our Help, as long as we live, and let the Lord do as seemeth good in his Eyes. But said she, Give me the heavenly Physician; He is the only Helper. Doth not he say, *Come unto me all ye that are weary and heavy laden, and I will give you Rest:* And doth not he bid us call upon him in the Day of Distress, and he will deliver us, and we shall glorify him: Therefore, dear Father, call upon him yet again for me.

27. About this Time a Christian Friend came in to visit her, who was not a little comforted when he heard and saw so much of the Grace of God living in a poor young Thing, which could not but so far affect him as to draw Tears of Joy and Admiration from him,

and her Deportment was so teaching, that he could not but acknowledge himself greatly edified and improved by her Carriage and Language.

28. That which was not the least observable in her, was the ardent Affection she had for the holy Scriptures and her Catechism, in which she was thro'ly instructed by the Divines of the Place where she lived, which she could not but own as one of the greatest Mercies next the Lord Christ. O how did she bless God for her Catechism, and beg of her Father to go particularly to those Ministers that had taken so much Pains with her to instruct her in her Catechism, and to thank them from her a dying Child for their good Instructions, and to let them understand, for their Encouragement to go on in the Work of Catechising, how refreshing those Truths were now to her in the Hour of her Distress. O that sweet Catechising, said she, unto which I did always resort with Gladness, and attended without Weariness.

29. She was much above the Vanities of the World, and took no Pleasure at a'l in those Things which usually take up the Heart and Time of young Ones. She would say, that she was grieved and ashamed both for Young and Old, to see how glad and mad they were upon Vanity, and how foolishly they spent their Time.

30. She was not forgetful of the Care and

Love of her Master and Mistress, who taught her to Read and Work, but she desired that Thanks might also be particularly given to them. Indeed she tho't she could never be thankful eno' both to God and Man for that Kindness that she had Experience of; But again and again, she desired to besure to thank the Ministers who instructed her, either by Catechising, or Preaching.

31. After some rest, her Father ask'd her again, How she did, and began to express somewhat of that Satisfaction and Joy that he had taken in her former Diligence, in her reading the Scriptures, and Writing, and her Dutifulness, and that great Progress she had made in the Things of God: Upon which she humbly and sweetly desired to own God and his Kindness in her godly Education, and said, she esteemed her holy Education under such Parents and Ministers, as a greater Portion than ten Thousand Gilders, for thereby I have learned to comfort my self out of the Word of God, which the World besides could never have afforded.

32. Her Father perceiving her to grow very weak, said, I perceive Child, thou art very weak; It is true Sir *(said she)* I feel my Weakness increaseth, and I see your Sorrow increasing too; which is a Piece of my Affliction: Be content I pray you. It is the Lord which doth it; and let you and I say with *David*,

Let us fall into the Lord's Hand, for his Mercies are great.

33. She laid a great Charge upon her Parents not to be over-grieved for her after her Death, urging that of *David* on them; while the Child was sick, he fasted and wept; but when it died, he washed his Face and sat up and eat, and said, *Can I bring him back again from Death? I shall go to him, but he shall not return to me.* So ought you to say after my Death, *Our Child is well*; for we know it shall be well with them that trust in the Lord. She did lay a more particular and strait Charge upon her Mother; saying to her, Dear Mother, who have done so much for me, you must promise me one Thing more before I die; and that is, That you will not sorrow overmuch for me: I speak thus to you, because I am afraid of your great Affliction. Consider others Losses, what they have been; remember *Job*; forget not what Christ foretold, *In the World you shall have Tribulation, but be of good Cheer, in me you shall have Peace*: And must the Apostles suffer so great Tribulation, and must we suffer none? Did not Jesus Christ, my only Life and Saviour, sweat Drops of Blood? Was he not in a bittter Agony, mocked, spit at, nailed to the Cross, and a Spear thrust thro' his bless'd Side; and all this for my sake, for my stinking sins sake? Did not he cry out, *My God, my God, why hast thou for-*

G

saken me? Did not Christ hang naked upon the Cross to purchase for me the Garments of Salvation, and to cloath me with his Righteousness, for there is Salvation in no other Name.

34. Being very feeble and weak, she said, O if I might quietly sleep in the Bosom of Jesus; and that till then he would strengthen me! O that he would take me into his Arms as he did those little Ones, where He said, *Suffer little Children to come unto me, for of such is the Kingdom of Heaven, and he took them into his Arms, and laid his Hands on them and blessed them.* I lie here as a Child, O Lord I am thy Child, receive me into thy gracious Arms. O Lord, Grace! Grace! and not Justice! for if thou shouldst enter into Judgment with me, I cannot stand, yea, none living should be just in thy Sight!

35. After this, she cried out, O how faint am I! But fearing least she should dishearten her Mother, she said, While there is Life, there is Hope: If it should please the Lord to recover me, how careful would I be to please you in my Work and Learning, and whatsoever you should require of me!

36. After this, the Lord did again send her Strength, and she laboured to spend it all for Christ, in the awakening, edifying and comforting of those who were about her; but her chiefest Endeavour was to support her dear Parents from extraordinary Sorrow, and to

comfort them out of the Scriptures, telling them, *That she knew that all Things did work together for the Good of them that did love God, even to those who are called according to his Purpose.* O God establish me with thy free Spirit! *Who shall separate us from the Love of Christ? I am perswaded that neither Life, nor Death, nor Angels, nor Principalities, nor Powers, nor Things present, nor Things to come, nor Height, nor any other Creature, shall separate us from the Love of God, which is towards us in Christ Jesus our Lord.* My Sheep (saith Christ) *hear my Voice, and I know them, and they follow me, and I give unto them eternal Life, and they shall never perish, and no Man shall pluck them out of my Hands. My Father who gave them me is greater than all, and none shall pluck them out of my Father's Hands.* Thus she seemed to attain to a holy Confidence in God, and an Assurance of her State as to another World.

37. When she had a little refeshed her self with Rest, she burst forth with Abundance of Joy & gladness of Heart, with a holy Triumph of Faith, saying out, *Death is swallowed up of Victory: O Death where is thy Sting! O Grave where is thy Victory! The Sting of Death is Sin, and the Strength of Sin is the law; but Thanks be to God who hath given us the Victory thro' our Lord and Saviour Jesus Christ.*

38. That she might the better support her Friends, she still insisted upon that which might take off some of their Burthen, by urging the

Neceſſity of Death: *We are from the Earth, and to the Earth we muſt return; Duſt is the Mother of us all, the Duſt ſhall return to the Duſt, from whence it is; and the Spirit to God who gave it.*

39. Then ſhe diſcourſed of the ſhortneſs of Man's Life. O what is the Life of Man! *The Days of Man upon the Earth are as the Graſs, and the Flowers of the Field, ſo he flouriſheth, the Wind paſſeth over it, and it is no more, and his Place knows him no more.*

40. She further urged the Sin and Sorrow that did attend us in this Life, and the longer we live, the more we ſin; now the Lord will free me from that Sin and Sorrow. We know not the Tho'ts of God, yet do we know ſo much, that they are Mercy and Peace, and do give an expected End. But what ſhall I ſay, my Life will not continue long, I feel much Weakneſs, O Lord, look upon me graciouſly, have Pity upon my weak diſtreſſed Heart. I am oppreſſed, undertake for me, that I may ſtand faſt and overcome.

41. She was very frequent in ſpiritual Ejaculations, and it was no ſmall Comfort to her, that the Lord Chriſt did pray for her, and promiſe to ſend his Spirit to comfort her. *It's ſaid* (ſaid ſhe) *I will pray the Father, and he ſhall give you another Comforter.* O let not him leave me! O Lord, continue with me till my Battle and Work be finiſhed.

42. She had very low and undervaluing

Tho'ts of herself, and her own Righteousness: What meant she else to cry out in such Language as that, *None but Christ!* Without Thee I can do Nothing! Christ is the true Vine! O let me be a Branch of that Vine! What poor Worms are we! O dear Father, how Lame and Halting do we go in the Ways of God and Salvation? We know but in Part, but when that which is perfect is come, then that which is imperfect shall be done away. O that I had attained to that now: But what are we our selves; not only Weakness and Nothingness, but Wickedness: For all the Tho'ts and Imaginations of Man's Heart, are only Evil, and that continually: We are by Nature Children of Wrath, and are conceived and born in Sin and Unrighteousness. Oh! Oh! this wretched and vile Thing *Sin!* But thanks to God who hath redeem'd me from it.

43. She comforted her self and her Father, in that great Scripture, Rom. 8. 15. 16, 17. *Ye have not received the Spirit of Bondage again to Fear, but ye have received the Spirit of Adoption, by which we cry* Abba Father. *It is the Spirit that witnesseth with our Spirits, that we are the Children of God; and if Children, then we are Heirs, Heirs of God, and Joint-Heirs with Christ.* You see thence Father, that I shall be a Fellow-Heir with Christ, who hath said, *In my Father's House are many Mansions, if it were not so, I would have told you, I go to prepare a*

Place for you, I will come again, and take you to my self, that where I am, there ye may be also. O Lord, take me to thy self. Behold, dear Mother, he hath prepared a Place and Dwelling for me.

44. Yea, my dear Child, said her Mother, He shall strengthen you with his holy Spirit, until he hath fitted and prepared you fully for that Place which he hath prepared for you.

45. Yea Mother, it is said in the Eighty fourth Psalm, *How lovely are thy Tabernacles, O Lord of Hosts, my Soul do thirst, and longeth for the Courts of the Lord: One Day in thy Courts is better than a Thousand; yea, I had rather be a Door-keeper in the House of God, than dwell in the Tents of the Wicked.* Read that Psalm, dear Mother, wherewith we may comfort one another. As for me, I am more and more spent, and draw near my last Hour.

46. Then she desired to be pray'd with, and begged that the Lord would give her an easy Passage.

47. After this, she turned to her Mother, and with much Affection, she said, Ah my dear and loving Mother; that which cometh from the Heart, doth ordinarily go to the Heart; once more come and kiss me before I leave you.

48. She was not a little concerned about the Souls of her Relations, and did particularly charge it upon her Father, to do what he possibly could to bring them up in the Ways of

God. O let my Sister be trained up in the Scriptures, and Catechising, as I have been.

49. I formerly wept for my Sister, thinking that she should die before me, and now she weepeth for me, and then she kissed her weeping Sister. Also she took her young little Sister in her Arms, a Child of six Months old, and she kissed it with much Affection, as if her very Bowels had moved within her, and spoke with many Heart-breaking Words, both to her Parents and the Children.

50. Her Father spake to one that was by, to take the poor little Child away from her, from the Hazard of that fiery Distemper, and bid his Daughter to take her from her, for he had already too much to bear. Well Father, said she, did not God preserve the three Children in the fiery Furnace: And did you not teach me that Scripture, *When thou passest thro' the Fire thou shalt not burn, neither shall the Flame kindle upon thee.*

51. She had a very strong Faith in the Doctrine of the Resurrection, and did greatly solace her Soul with excellent Scriptures, which do speak the happy State of Believers, as soon as their Souls are separated from their Bodies; and what she quoted out of the Scriptures, she did excellently and suitably apply to her own Use, incomparably above the common Reach of her Sex and Age. That in 1 *Cor.* 15. 42. was a good Support to her. The Body *is sown in Corruption, but it shall be raised.*

*Incorruptible; It is sown in dishono[r]
raised in Glory: It is sown in Wea[kness]
shall be raised in Power.* And then [she]
applies, and takes in this Cordia[l]
thus it is, and thus it shall be wi[th]
mortal Flesh: *Blessed are the Dea[d in]
the Lord, because they rest from th[eir Labours,]
and their Works do follow them.*
[Righte]ous perish, and no Man layeth it t[o heart,]
the Upright are taken away, and no [one consider]-
eth it, that they are taken away f[rom the evil]
to come; They shall enter into Pe[ace, they]
shall rest in their Beds, every one wh[o walks in]
their Uprightness. Behold now Fa[ther, you shall]
rest and sleep in that Bed-Chamb[er.]

52. Then she quoted Job 19. *I know that my Redeemer liveth, [and he]
shall stand at the latter End upon [the Earth,]
and tho' after my Skin Worms destr[oy this Body,]
yet in my Flesh shall I see God; [whom I shall]
see for my self, and my Eyes shall be[hold and not]
anothers, tho' my Reins be consume[d.]*
Behold now Father, this very Ski[n which you]
see, and this very Flesh which you [see, shall be]
raised up again; and these very [Eyes, which]
now are so dim, shall on that Day [see and be]-
hold my dear and precious Redee[mer; tho']
the Worms eat up my Flesh, ye[t with these]
Eyes shall I behold God, even I [my self, and]
not another for me.

53. Then she quoted Joh. 5. [Marvel]
not at this, for the Hour is coming

that are in their Graves shall come forth; those that have done Good unto the Resurrection of Life. See Father, I shall rise in that Day, and then I shall behold my Redeemer; then shall he say, *Come ye blessed of my Father, inherit the Kingdom prepared for you before the Beginning of the World.*

54. *Behold now I live, yet not I, but Christ liveth in me, and the Life that I now live in the Flesh, is by the Faith of the Son of God, who loved me, and gave himself for me. I am saved, and that not of my self, it is the Gift of God, not of Works, that no Man should boast.*

55. My dear Parents, now we must shortly part, my Speech faileth me, pray the Lord for a quiet Close to my Combat.

56. Her Parents replied, Ah our dear Child, how sad is that to us, that we must part? She answered, I go to Heaven, and there we shall find one another again; I go to Jesus Christ.

57. Then she comforted her self to think of seeing her precious Brother and Sister again in Glory. I go to my Brother *Jacob,* who did so much cry and call upon God to the last Moment of his Breath: And to my little Sister, who was but three Years old when she died: Who, when we asked her, Whether she would die? Answered, *Yes, if it be the Lord's Will. I will go to my little Brother, if it be the Lord's Will, or I will stay with my Mother, if it be the Lord's Will. But I know that I shall die, and go to Heaven and to God.* O see, how so small

a Babe had so much given it to behave it self every Way, and in all Things so submissively to the Will of God, as if it had no Will of its own; but if it be the Will of God, if it please God; nothing from her, but what is the Will and Pleasure of God: And therefore dear Father and Mother, give the Lord Thanks for this his free and rich Grace, and then I shall the more gladly be gone. Be gracious then, O Lord, unto me also, be gracious to me. Wash me throughly from my Unrighteousness, and cleanse me from my Sin.

58. After this, her Spirit was refreshed with the Sense of the Pardon of her Sins, which made her to cry out, Behold God hath washed away my Sins, O how do I long to die! The Apostle said, *In this Body we earnestly sigh and groan, longing for our House which is in Heaven, that we may be cloathed therewith.* Now I also lie here sighing and longing for that Dwelling which is above. In the last Sermon which I heard or ever shall hear, I heard this in the New-Church, which is Matter of great Comfort to me.

59. Then she repeated several notable Scriptures which were quoted in that Sermon, afterwards she desired to be pray'd with, and put Petitions into their Mouths, *viz.* That all her Sins might be forgiven, That she might have more abundant Faith, and the Assurance of it; and the Comfort of that Assurance, and the Continuation and Strength of that

Comfort, according as her Neceffity fhould require. Afterwards fhe prayed herfelf, and continued pretty Space.

60. When Prayers were ended, fhe called to her Father and Mother, and demanded of them, whether fhe had at any Time anger'd or griev'd them, or done any Thing that did not become her? And begged of them to forgive her.

61. They anfwered her, that if all Children had carried themfelves fo to their Parents as fhe had done, there would be lefs Grief and Sorrow on all Hands than there is; and if any Thing hath efcaped thee, we would forgive it with all our Hearts, you have done as became a good Child.

62. Her Heart being quieted with her Peace with God and her Parents, fhe began to difpofe of her Books; particularly fhe intreated her Mother to keep Mr. *De Wit*'s Catechife Lectures, as long as fhe lived, for her Sake, and let my little Sifter have my other Books as my Remembrance.

63. Then (faid fhe) fhe felt her Breaft exceedingly pained, by which fhe knew that her End was very nigh. Her Father fpake to her as he was able, telling her the Lord would be her Strength in the Hour of her Neceffity.

64. Yea faid fhe, *The Lord is my Shepherd, altho' I pafs thro' the Valley of the Shadow of Death, I will not fear, for thou art with me, thy Rod and thy Staff, they comfort me:* And

it is said, *The Sufferings of this present Life, are not worthy to be compared with the Glory that shall be revealed in us.* Shall I not suffer and endure, seeing my glorious Redeemer was pleas'd to suffer so much for me? O how was He mocked and crowned with Thorns, that he might purchase a Crown of Righteousness for us: And that is the Crown of which *Paul* spoke, when he said, *I have fought the good Fight, I have finished my Course, I have kept the Faith; henceforth is laid up for me a Crown of Righteousness, which the Lord the righteous Judge, shall give unto me in that Day; and not only unto me, but to all that love his Appearing.*

65. *Ye are bought with a Price, therefore glorify God with your Souls and Bodies, which are his.* Must I not then exalt and bless Him while I have a Being, who hath bought me with his Blood! *Surely he hath borne our Griefs, and took our Infirmities, and we esteemed Him smitten and stricken of God: But he was wounded for our Transgressions, and bruised for our Sins: The Chastisement of our Peace was upon Him, and by his Stripes we are healed; and the Lord laid upon Him the Iniquity of us all.* Behold the Lamb of God that taketh away the Sins of the World: That Lamb is Jesus Christ, who hath satisfied for my Sins. So saith *Paul, Ye are washed, ye are sanctified, ye are justified in the Name of our Lord Jesus, and thro' the Spirit of our God.*

66. My End is now very near, now I shall

put on white Raiment, and be cloathed before the Lamb, that spotless Lamb, and with his spotless Righteousness. Now are the Angels making ready to carry my Soul before the Throne of God. *These are they who are come out of great Tribulation, who have washed their Robes, and made them white in the Blood of the Lamb.*

67. She spoke this with a dying Voice, but full of Spirit, and of the Power of Faith.

68. Her lively Assurance she further uttered in the Words of the Apostle, *We know that if this earthly House of our Tabernacle be dissolved, we have one which is built of God, which is eternal in the Heavens; for in this, we sigh for our House which is in Heaven, that we may be cloathed therewith.*

69. There Father, you see that my Body is this Tabernacle, which now shall be broken down: my Soul shall now part from it, and shall be taken up into that heavenly Paradise, into that heavenly *Jerusalem.* There shall I dwell and go no more out, but sit and sing. *Holy, holy, holy, is the Lord God of Hosts, the Lord of Sabbath!* Her last Words were these: *O Lord God, into thy Hands I commit my Spirit, O Lord be gracious, be merciful to me a poor Sinner.*------

And here she fell asleep.

70. She died the first of *September* 1664, betwixt Seven and Eight in the Evening! in

the Fourteenth Year of her Age; having obtain'd that which she so oft intreated of the Lord, a quiet and easy Departure, and the End of her Faith, the Salvation of her Soul.

EXAMPLE XII.

Of the excellent Carriage of a Child upon his Death-Bed, when but Seven Years old.

1. Jacob Bicks, the Brother of *Susannah Bicks*, was born in *Leiden*, in the Year 1657; and had religious Education, under his godly Parents, the which the Lord was pleased to sanctify to his Conversion, and by it lay in excellent Provisions to live upon in an Hour of Distress.

2. This sweet little Child was visited of the Lord of a very sore Sickness, upon the sixth of *August* 1664, three or four Weeks before his Sister, of whose Life and Death, we have given you some Account already: In this Distemper he was for the most Part very sleepy and drowsy, till near his Death, but when he did awake, he was won't still to fall a praying.

3. Once when his Parents had prayed with him, they asked him if they should once more send for the Physician; *No* (said he) *I will have the Doctor no more; the Lord will help me; I know He will take me to Himself, and then he shall help all.*

4. Ah my dear Child, said his Father, tha

Heart; *Well,* (said the Child) *pray, and the Lord shall be near.*

his Parents had prayed with him
d, *Come now dear Father and Mo-
me, I know that I shall die.*
d dear Father and Mother. Fare-
er, Farewel all. Now shall I go
nto God and Jesus Christ, and the
: Father, know you not what is
niah; *Blessed is he who trusted in*
Now I trust in him, and he will
And in 1 *Joh.* 2. it is said, *Little*
e not the World, for the World pas-

then all that is in the World, away
 pleasant Things in the World:
y Dagger, for where I go, there
o do with Daggers and Swords:
not fight there, but praise God,
ll my Books; there shall I know
 and be learned in all Things of
n, without Books.
ather being touched to hear his
 at this Rate, could not well tell
; but my dear Child, the Lord
thee, and uphold thee.
ather (*said he*) the Apostle *Peter*
isteth the Proud, but he giveth Grace
le. I shall humble my self under
Hand of God, and he will help
up.

10. O my dear Child, said his Father, hast thou so strong a Faith?

11. *Yes*, said the Child, God hath given me so strong a Faith upon Himself thro' Jesus Christ, that the Devil himself shall flee from me, for it is said, *He that believeth in the Son hath Everlasting Life, and he hath overcome the wicked One.* Now I believe in Jesus Christ my Redeemer, and he will not leave or forsake me, but shall give unto me eternal Life, and then shall I sing, *Holy, holy, holy, is the Lord of Sabbath.*

12. Then with a short Word of Prayer, *Lord be merciful to me a poor Sinner*, he quietly breathed out his Soul, and sweetly slept in Jesus, when he was about Seven Years old. He died *August* the 8th 1664.

HALLELUJAH.

EXAMPLE XIII.

Of One who began to look towards Heaven, when he was very Young, with many eminent Passages of his Life, and his joyful Death, when he was Eleven Years and three Quarters old.

1. JOhn Harvy was born in *London*, in the Year 1654. His Father was a Dutch Merchant. He was piously Educated under his virtuous Mother; and soon began to suck in divine Things with no small Delight.

2. The first Thing very observable in him

was, that when he was two Years and eight Months old, he could speak as well as other Children do usually at five Years old.

3. His Parents judging, that he was then a little too Young to send out to School, let him have his Liberty to Play a little about their Yard. But instead of playing, he found out a School of his own Accord hard by Home, and went to the School-Mistress, and intreated her to teach him to read, and so went for some Time to School without the Knowledge of his Parents, and made a very strange Progress in his Learning, and was able to read distinctly, before most Children are able to know their Letters.

4. He was wont to ask many serious and weighty Questions, about Matters which concerned his Soul and Eternity.

5. His Mother being greatly troubled upon the Death of one of his Uncles, this Child came to his Mother, and said, " Mother, tho'
" my Uncle be dead, doth not the Scripture
" say, he must rise again : Yea, and I must
" die, and so must every Body; and it will not
" be long before Christ will come to Judge
" the World; and then we shall see one ano-
" ther again, I pray Mother, do not weep so
" much." This grave Counsel he gave his Mother, when he was not quite five Years old, by which her Sorrow for her Brother was turned into Admiration at her Child, and she was

made to sit silent and quiet under that smarting Stroke.

6. After this, his Parents removed to *Aberdeen* in *Scotland*, and settled their Child under an able and painful School-Master there, whose Custom was upon the Lord's Day in the Morning, to examine his Scholars concerning the Sermons that they had heard the former Lord's Day, and to add some other Questions which might try the Understanding and Knowledge of his Scholars; the Question that was once proposed to his Form was, *Whether God had a Mother?* None of all the Scholars could Answer it, till it came to *John Harvy*, who being asked, *Whether God had a Mother?* Answered, *No, as He was God, He could not have a Mother; but as He was Man He had.* This was before he was quite six Years old. His Master was somewhat amazed at the Child's Answer, and took the first Opportunity to go to his Mother, to thank her for instructing her Son so well; but she replied, that he was never taught that from her, but that he understood it by Reading, and his own Observation.

7. He was a Child that was extraordinary inquisitive, and full of good Questions, and very careful to observe and remember what he heard.

8. He had a great Hatred of whatsoever he knew to be displeasing to God, and was so greatly concerned for the Honour of God, that

he would take on bitterly if any gross Sins were committed before him. And he had a deep Sense of the Worth of Souls, and was not a little grieved when he saw any do that which he knew was dangerous to their Souls.

9. One Day seeing one of his near Relations come into his Father's House distempered with Drink, as he thought, he quickly went very seriously to him, and wept over him, that he should so offend God, and hazard his Soul, and begged of him to spend his Time better than in Drinking and Gaming; and this he did, without any Instruction from his Parents, but from an inward Principle of Grace, and Love to God and Souls, as it is verily believed.

10. When he was at Play with other Children, he would be oftentimes putting in some Word to keep them from naughty Talk or wicked Actions; and if any did take the Lord's Name in vain, or do any Thing that was not becoming of a Child, they should soon hear of it with a Witness; nay, once hearing a Boy speak very prophanely, and that after two or three Admonitions, he would not forbear, nor go out of his Company neither, he was so transported with Zeal, that he could not forbear falling upon him to beat him, but his Mother chiding him for it, he said, that he could not endure to hear the Name of God so abused by a wretched Boy.

This is observed not to vindicate the Act, but to take Notice of his Zeal.

11. He was a Child that took great Delight in the Company of good Men, and especially Ministers and Scholars; and if he had any leisure Time, he would improve it by visiting of such, whose Discourse might make him wiser and better; and when he was in their Society, to be sure, his Talk was more like a Christian and Scholar than a Child.

12. One Day after School time was over, he gave Mr. *Andrew Kent* (one of the Ministers of *Aberdeen*) a Visit, and asked him several solid Questions, but the good Man asked him some Questions out of his Catechism, and find him not so ready in the Answers as he should have been, did a little reprove him, and told him, that he must be sure to get his Catechism perfectly by Heart: The Child took the Reproof very well, and went Home, and fell very hot upon his Catechism, and never left, tell he had got it by Heart; and not only so, but he would be enquiring into the Sense and Meaning of it.

13. He was so greatly taken with his Catechism, that he was not content to learn it himself, but he would be putting others upon learning their Catechism, especially those that were nearest him; He could not be satisfied, till he had perswaded his Mother's Maids to learn it; and when they were at Work, he would be still following them with some good Question or other; so that the Child seemed to be taken up with the Tho'ts of his Soul, and

God's Honour, and the good of other Souls.

14. He was a confciencious obferver of the Lord's Day, fpending all the Time either in fecret Prayer, or reading the Scriptures, and good Books; Learning of his Catechifm, and hearing the Word of God, and publick Duties; and was not only careful in the Performance of thefe Duties himfelf, but was ready to put all that he knew upon a ftrict Obfervation of the Lord's Day, and was exceedingly grieved at the Prophanation of it. One Lord's Day, a Servant of his Father's going out of the Houfe upon extraordinary Occafion, to fetch fome Beer, he took on fo bitterly, that he could fcarce be pacified becaufe that holy Day was fo abufed (as he judged) in his Father's Houfe.

15. When he was between fix and feven Years old; it pleafed God to afflict him with fore Eyes, which was no fmall Grief to him, becaufe it kept him from School, which he loved as well as many Boys do their Play: and that which was worfe, he was commanded by the Doctor not to read any Book whatfoever at home. But, O how was this poor Child grieved, that he might not have Liberty to read the holy Scriptures; and for all their Charge, he would get by himfelf, and ftand by the Window, and read the Bible and good Books; yea, he was fo greedy of reading the Scriptures, and took fo much Delight in them, that he would fcarce allow Time to drefs himfelf; for reading the Word of God was his

great Delight. Yea, tho' he had been, beat for studying so much, yet judging it God's Command, that he should give himself up to reading, he could not be beat off from it, till he was so bad, that he had like never to have recovered his Sight more.

16. It was his Practice to be much by himself in secret Prayer, and he was careful to manage that Work, so as that it might be as secret as possible it could be, but his frequency and constancy made it to be easily observed; upon which, a Person having a great Mind to know what this sweet Babe prayed for, got into a Place near him, and heard him very earnestly praying for the Church of God, desiring that the Kingdom of the Gospel might be spread over the whole World, and that the Kingdom of Grace might more and more come into the Hearts of God's People, and that the Kingdom of Glory might be hastened. He was won't to continue half an Hour, sometimes an Hour together upon his Knees.

17. He was much above the Vanities that most Children are taken with, and was indeed too much a Man to live long.

18. He was very humble and modest, and did by no Means affect fineness in Apparel, but hated any Thing more than Necessaries, either in Cloaths or Diet.

19. When he perceived either his Brother or Sisters pleased with their new Cloaths, he would with a great deal of Gravity reprove their Fol-

[95]

…n his Reproof signified little, he
…il their Vanity.

…he had a new Suit brought from
…, which when he looked on, he
…Ribbons at the Knees, at which
…ed; asking his Mother, *Whether
…would keep him warm?* No Child,
…her; *Why then* (said he) *do you suf-
…be put here; you are mistaken, if
…ch Things please me; and I doubt
…better than us, may want the Money
…you, to buy them Bread.*

…vould intreat his Mother to have a
…tifying a proud Humour in his
…Sisters; he did tell them of the
…Pride, and how little Reason they
…oud of that which was their Shame;
…*If it had not been for Sin, we should
…Need of Cloaths.*

…easure Time, he would be talking
…ol-Fellows about the Things of
…rge the Necessity of a holy Life.
…e much spoke on to them, *The Ax
…Root of the Tree, and every Tree
…not forth good Fruit, is hewn down
…the Fire.* Every Mother's Child
…oth not bring forth the Fruit of
…s, shall shortly be cut down with
…od's Wrath, and cast into the Fire
…d this he spake like One that be-
…elt the Power of what he spake,
…h the least Visibility of a childish

Levity of Spirit. This was, when he was between Seven and Eight Years old, and if he perceived any Children unconcerned about their Souls he would be greatly troubled at it.

23. After this, his Parents removed not far from *London*, where he continued 'till that dreadful Year Sixty-five: He was then sent to the *Latin* School, where he soon made a great Progress, and was greatly beloved of his Master, the School was his beloved Place, and Learning his Recreation. He was never taught to write, but took it of his own Ingenuity.

24. He was exceeding dutiful to his Parents, and never did in the least dispute their Command, except, when he tho't they might cross the Command of God, (as in the forementioned Business of reading the Scriptures when his Eyes were so bad.)

25. He was exceedingly contented with any mean Diet, and to be sure he would not touch a Bit of any Thing, 'till he had begged God's Blessing upon it.

26. He would put his Brother and Sisters upon their Duties, and observe them whether they performed it or no, and when he saw any neglect, he would soon warn them; if he saw any of them take a Spoon into their Hands before they had craved a Blessing, He said, *That is just like a Hog indeed.*

27. His Sister was afraid of the Darkness, and would sometimes cry, upon this Account;

he told her, *She must fear God more, and she need then be afraid of nothing.*

28. He would humbly put his near Relations upon their Duty, and minding the Concerns of their Souls and Eternity, with more Seriousness and Life; and to have a Care of doing of that which was for the Dishonour of God, and the Hazard of the Soul.

29. He was of a compassionate and charitable Disposition, and very pitiful to the Poor, or any that were in Distress, but his greatest Pity was to poor Souls; and as well as he could, he would be putting Children, Play-Fellows, Servants and Neighbours, upon minding their poor Souls.

30. One notable Instance of his true Charity, I cannot omit. A certain Turk was by the Providence of God, cast into the Place where he lived, which this sweet Child hearing of, had a great Pity to his Soul, and studied how he might be any way instrumental to do it Good; at last, finding a Man that understood the Language of the *Turk*, he used Means to get them together, which he at last procured; the first Thing that he did, was to put his Friend upon discoursing with the *Turk* about his Principles, whether he acknowledged a Deity; which the *Turk* owning, the next Thing he enquired after, was, *What he thought of the Lord Jesus Christ.* At which the *Turk* was troubled, and put off the Discourse, and

I

said, he was athirst, and an hungry; which the Child being informed of, by the Interpreter, immediately went to a Brew-House near at Hand (his own House being far off) and did intreat the Master of the Brew-House to give him some Beer for the *Turk*, and the Argument he used was this, *Sir, here is a poor Stranger that is athirst, we know not where we may be cast before we die:* He went to another Place, and begged Food for him; using the same Argument as before. But his Friends hearing of it, were angry with him, but he told them he did it for a poor Stranger that was far from Home; and he did it, that he might think the better of the Christians, and the Christian Religion.

31. He would have a savoury Word to say to every one he conversed with, to put them in Mind of the Worth of Christ, and their Souls, and their nearness to Eternity. Insomuch, that good People took no small Pleasure in his Company. The Taylor that made his Cloathes, would keep them the longer before he brought them Home, that he might have the Benefit of his spiritual and christian Society; and more frequent Visits.

32. He bewailed the miserable Condition of the Generality of Mankind (when he was about ten Years old) that were utterly estranged from God, tho' they called him Father, yet they were his Children only by Creation, and

not by any Likeness they had to God, or Interest in Him.

33. Thus he continued walking in the Ways of God, engaged in reading, praying, hearing the Word of God, and spiritual Discourse, discovering thereby his serious Thoughts of Eternity.

34. He had an earnest Desire if it might be the Lord's good Pleasure, to give himself up to the Lord in the Work of the Ministry, if he should live; and this out of a dear Love to Christ and Souls.

35. He was next to the Bible, most taken with reading of the Rev. Mr. *Baxter*'s Works, especially his *Saints Everlasting Rest*; and truly, the Thoughts of that Rest, and Eternity, seemed to swallow up all other Thoughts, and he lived in a constant Preparation for it, and looked more like one that was ripe for Glory, than an Inhabitant of this lower World.

36. When he was about eleven Years and three Quarters old, his Mother's House was visited with the Plague: his eldest Sister was the first that was visited with this Distemper, and when they were praying for her, he would sob and weep bitterly.

37. As soon as he perceived that his Sister was dead, he said, *The Will of the Lord be done: Blessed be the Lord. Dear Mother*, said he, *you must do as David did, after the Child was dead, he went and refreshed himself, and quietly submitted himself to the Will of God.*

38. The rest of the Family held well for about fourteen Days, which Time he spent in religious Duties, and preparing for his Death; but still his great Book was, *The Saints Rest*; which he read with exceeding Curiosity, gathering many Observations out of it in Writing, for his own Use. He wrote several divine Meditations of his own upon several Subjects; but that which seemest most admirable was a Meditation upon the Excellency of Christ: He was never well but when he was more immediately engaged in the Service of God.

39. At fourteen Days End, he was taken sick, at which he seemed very patient and chearful, yet sometimes he would say that his Pain was great.

40. His Mother looking upon his Brother, shaked her Head; at which he asked, if his Brother were marked: she answered, *Yea Child*, he asked again, whether he were marked; she answered nothing: *Well*, says he, *I know I shall be marked*; *I pray let me have Mr. Baxter's Book, that I may read a little more of Eternity, before I go into it.* His Mother told him, That he was not able to read: He said that he was; however then pray by me and for me: His Mother answered, she was so full of Grief, that she could not pray now; but she desired to hear him pray his last Prayer.

41. His Mother asked him, whether he were willing to die, and leave her? He answered,

…illing to leave you, and go to my …er. His Mother answered, *Child,* …but an *Assurance of God's Love,* I …so much troubled.

…nswered, and said to his Mother, …dear Mother, that my Sins are for‑ …at I shall go to Heaven; for, said …d an Angel by me, that told me, I …be in Glory.

…is his Mother burst forth into …Mother, said he, *did you but know* …feel, *you would not weep, but rejoyce.* …m *so full of Comfort, that I can't* …I am; O Mother, I shall presently …d in my Father's Bosom, and shall …re the four and twenty Elders shall …eir Crowns, and sing Hallelujah, …raise, to Him that sits upon the …nto the Lamb for ever.

… this, his Speech began to fail …Soul seemed still to be taken up …nd nothing now grieved him but …that he saw his Mother to be in …h; a little to divert his Mother, …*What she had to Supper*; but pre‑ …kind of divine Rapture, he cried …*sweet Supper have I making ready* …*ory!*

…eeing all this rather increase, than …ther's Grief, he was more troubled, …er what she meant, thus to offend

God; know you not, that it is the Hand of the Almighty. *Humble your self under the mighty Hand of God. Lay your self in the Dust, and kiss the Rod of God, and let me see you do it, in Token of your Submission to the Will of God, and bow before Him.* Upon which, raising himself a little, he gave a lowly Bow, and spoke no more, but went chearfully and triumphingly to rest, in the Bosom of JESUS.

• *HALLELUJAH.*

A NARRATIVE of sundry Remarkable Passages concerning Mr. *John Langham,* Son of Sir JAMES LANGHAM, Knight and Baronet.

By THOMAS BURROUGHS, *B. D.*

THis sweet Child was *five Years* and an *half* old within two or three Days, when God took him: But he had arrived to that in five Years, and a little more, that some (I am afraid) have not arrived to in ten Times the Space.*

He had learnt the *Assemblies shorter Catechism* thro', and began to learn it over again, with the Proofs out of the Scriptures at large, wherein he had made some Progress.

He met one Day (in a Gentlewoman's Chamber, who lives in the House) with a *Book* that treated of the *Passion* of CHRIST, and reading a little in it, said he liked the Book well, and that he would read it over. So he began

* *He died* July 29, 1659.

and read some few Pages, then turned the Leaf down, and the next Day came again and began where he left, and so from Day to Day, till he had read a considerable Part of it.

He was a very dutiful Child to his Parents, and would exceedingly rejoice, when he had done any Thing, or carried himself so, as to please them.

He was taken with the *Book* called, *The Practice of Piety,* and delighted to be reading in it.

His Father speaking to him one Day about the Devil and Hell, and Things of that Nature, asked him, If he were not afraid to be alone? He answered, *No: for God would defend him.* His Father asked, why he thought so? He replied, that *He loved God, and that he hoped that God loved him.* But (saith his Father) you have been a Sinner, and God loves not Sinners. *But I am sorry for my Sins* (saith he) *and do repent.* Repent (replied his Father) do you know what Repentance means, and what belongs to it? And he gave him a good Account of the Apprehension he had of the Nature of that Grace, according to what he had learned in his Catechism, but yet in his own Words and Expressions.

He would oft ask his Sister (who was somewhat younger than himself) *Whether she trusted in God, and loved God?* and would tell her, that, *If she sought God, God would be found of her; but if she forsook God, God would cast her off for ever.*

He took that Delight in his Book, that his Father and Mother have seen Cause sometimes to hide away his Book from him.

He was never observed to discover any Pouting or Discontent, when upon any Occasion he was corrected. And you must not think I am telling you the Story of one, in whom *Adam* (as they feign of *Bonaventure*) never sinned. There is *that Foolishness bound up in all Children's Hearts, that will sometimes need the Rod of Correction*; tho' there be very few in whom there appeared less than in him.

The Day before he died, He desired me to pray for him: I told him, If he would have me to pray for him, he must tell me, what I should pray for; and what he would have God to do for him! He answered, *To pardon his Sins*.

Oft upon his sick Bed he would be repeating to himself the 55th Chapter of *Isaiah*, and other Pieces of Scripture; which in the Time of his Health he had learned by Heart.

But that Passage in the forementioned Chapter was most frequently in his Mouth, and uttered by him with much Affection: *My Thoughts are not your Thoughts; neither are my Ways your Ways, saith the Lord: For as the Heavens are higher than the Earth, so are my Ways and my Thoughts than your Thoughts*: As if God (out of this sweet *Babe's-Mouth*) had, in these Words, read to his Parents a Lecture of Silence and Submission under *his Hand*; and taught them that he must be dealt with!

and difpofed of, not as they, but as his heavenly Father (whofe Thoughts were far different) fhould fee fitting.

One Time he broke out into this Expreffion; *My God, my God, deliver me out of this Mifery, and from the Pains of Hell for ever.*

A little before his Death he broke out into thefe Words; *My Sins pardon, my Soul fave, for Chrift his Sake.*

I cannot blame thofe worthy Perfons fo nearly related to him, though they mourn at parting with fuch a fweet and hopeful Child; any more than I could blame them for feeling Pain, if one of their Limbs were torn from another. Only they muft not mourn to Defpondency.

What an Inftrument of God's Glory might he have proved? What a deal of Service might he have done for God (in all Likelihood) had he lived to old Age? But it was God's doing.

A TOKEN
FOR THE
CHILDREN
OF
NEW-ENGLAND.

IF the Children of New-England *should not with an* Early Piety, *set themselves to* Know *and* Serve *the* Lord JESUS CHRIST, *the* GOD *of* their Fathers, *they will be condemned, not only by the* Examples *of* pious Children *in other Parts of the World, the publish'd and printed Accounts whereof have been brought over hither ; but there have been* Exemplary Children *in the Midst of New-England itself, that will rise up against them for their Condemnation. It would be a very profitable Thing to our* Children, *and highly acceptable to all the godly* Parents *of the* Children, *if, in Imitation of the excellent* JANEWAY's Token for Children, *there were made a* true Collection *of notable Things, exemplified in the* Lives *and* Deaths *of many among us, whose* Childhood *hath been signalized for what is virtuous and laudable.*

In the Church-History *of* New-England *is to be found the* Lives *of many eminent Persons, among whose Eminencies, not the least was,* Their fearing of the Lord from their Youth, *and their being* loved by the Lord when they were Children

But among the many other Instances, of a Childhood *and* Youth *delivered from* Vanity *by* serious Religion, *which* New-England *has afforded, these few have particularly been preserved*

EXAMPLE I.

LITTLE more than Thirteen Years old, was JOHN CLAP of *Scituate*, when he died; but it might very truly be said of him, *That while he was yet Young, he began to seek after the God of his Father.* From his Infancy he discovered a singular Delight in the holy Scriptures, whereby he was made *wise unto Salvation*; and also made himself yet further Amiable by his *Obedience* to his Parents, and his *Courtesy* to all his Neighbours. As he grew up, he signalized his Concern for Eternity, not only by his diligent Attendance upon both publick and private *Catechising*, but also by the like Attendance on the *Ministry of the Word*, which he would ponder and apply, and confer about with much Discretion of Soul, and *pray* for the good Effect thereof upon his own Soul. Yea, 'twas even from his Childhood observable in him, that ever after he began to speak reasonably, he would both affectionately regard the *Family Prayers*, and likewise, both Morning and Evening, with a most unwearied Constancy recommend himself by his own *Prayers* unto the Mercies of God.

Arriving higher into his Age, he was very conscientious of his Duty both to God and Man; and particularly careful of his Father's *Business*, which now became his own *Calling*. At Work with his Father in the Field, he

would frequently be propounding
by the Answers of which he mi[ght]
moted in the Knowledge of God
Seasons which others usually em[ploy]
Purposes, he would be abounding
ercises of Devotion. But of all
Things to be seen in him, he wa[s]
for nothing more than his Endea[vours]
paration for, and *Sanctification* o[f the]
Day. Yea, his Parents have affir[med]
a Year or two before he died, *The[re]*
an unprofitable Word come out of
but he would often bewail the i[dle]
vain Discourses of other People.

About a Year and a half before
good Spirit of God blessed him,
more thorough Conviction of hi[s]
Reason of *Sin* both *Original* & *Actu[al]*
tho' he had been such a *Pattern*
yet he would aggravate his own Si[n]
Lamentations truly extraordinary
his Relief against the *Terrors* of [God]
with he was now *distracted,* he v[as]
unto an utter Despair of his own
nesses and Abilities; but in this
he came to adore the Grace of G[od]
JESUS who is *able to save unto th[e]*
In his Longings to enjoy the L[ord]
thro' *Jesus,* he was like the *Hart* [after]
the Water-Brooks!

The Wounds of his *Spirit* we[re]
nied with a languishing and cons[umptive]

Flesh; yet with great Patience he endured the Hand of God, and he followed the Lord with *Prayers*, with *Cries*, with *Tears* for the Manifestation of the divine Love unto him.

It was also observed and admired, that when he was Abroad at the publick Worship, in the Time of his Weakness, he would *stand* the whole Time of the long Exercises, and be so affectionately attentive, that one might see every Sentence uttered in those Exercises, make some Impression upon him. The best *Christians* in the Place professed themselves made shamed by the Fervency of this *young Disciple!* And in Days of publick *Humiliations* or *Thanksgivings*, kept with Regard unto the general Circumstances of the Country, he would bear his Part, with such a Sense of the publick *Troubles* or *Mercies*, as argued more than a common Measure of a publick *Spirit* in him.

The Minister of the Place, visiting of him, after Sickness had confined him, found him in extream Dejection of Soul; his very Body shook, thro' his Fear, lest the *Day of Grace* were over with him; yet justifying of God, though he should be forever cast among the Damned. But yet his *Fears* were accompanied with *Hopes* in the Allsufficient Merits of the blessed *Jesus*: in which *Hopes* he continued using all the *Means of Grace*, according to his Capacity, and lamenting after those whereof he was not capable.

A Month before he died he kept his Bed;

the firſt *Fortnight* whereof he was very comfortleſs, and yet very *patient*: abounding all this while in gracious Admonitions unto other young People, that they would be concerned for their own eternal Salvation. And you ſhould not now have heard him complain, that he wanted *Health* and Eaſe, though he did ſo; but that he wanted *Faith*, and *Peace*, and *Chriſt*; yet expreſſing a profound Submiſſion to the Will of God. But in the laſt *Fortnight* of his Life, this poor Child of God, had his weary Soul more comfortably ſatiated with the *Promiſes* of the *New-Covenant*. God filled him with a marvellous Aſſurance of his Love, and ſo *ſealed* him with his own *Spirit* that he *rejoiced with Joy unſpeakable and full of Glory*. He would often be ſaying, *Whom have I in Heaven but thee? and there is none on Earth, that I deſire beſides thee: My Fleſh and my Heart faileth, but God is the Strength of my Heart, and my Portion for ever*. And, *I know that my Redeemer lives, and that he ſhall ſtand at the latter Day upon the Earth*. And, *If I live, I ſhall live unto the Lord; if I die, I ſhall die unto the Lord; and whether I live or die, I am the Lords*. And, *When Chriſt, who is my Life, ſhall appear, then ſhall I alſo appear with him in Glory*. He would profeſs that his Communion with the Lord Jeſus Chriſt, was *inexpreſſible*; and the Spectators judg'd his Conſolations, to be as great, as could be borne, in a mortal Body. Being now aſked, *Whether the*

Thoughts of dying troubled him not? He replied, *No, Death is no Terror to me, because Christ has taken away my Sin, which is the Sting of Death.* But being asked, *Whether he was willing to live?* He answered, *I am willing to submit unto the Will of God; but if God have appointed me to Life, I desire I may live to his Glory.* And being asked, *Whether God had put out of Doubt his Interest in a dying and rising Jesus?* He returned *Yes; and God has fully answered my Desires; I am now going to a thousand Times better World.* He told his Mother, *I love you as dearly as my own Life, yet I had rather die, and be with Christ.*

He continued six Days with his Teeth so shut, as that they could not be opened; and for the first *three Days* and Nights, he took no Sustenance; afterwards, tho' this but seldom, he sucked in between his Teeth, nothing but a little *cold Water*: in which Time, they that laid their Ears to his Lips, could overhear him continually expressing his Comfort in God. But just before his Death, his Teeth were opened; when he would often say, *Oh! how precious is the Blood of Christ, it is worth more than a thousand Worlds!* and often pray, *Come Lord Jesus, come quickly!* And at last, he gave up himself to God, in those Words, *Lord Jesus receive my Spirit.* He desired his Mother to turn his Face unto the Wall; whereupon she said, *John, Dost thou now re-*

member Hezekiah's *turning his Face unto the Wall?* He said, *Yes, I do remember it*: and as she turned him in her Arms, he quietly breathed his Soul into the Arms of his blessed Saviour.

[*Extracted out of the Account written and printed by* Mr. Witheril *and Mr.* Baker, *Ministers of* Scituate; *and preface'd by* Mr. Urian Oakes; *who takes that Occasion to say of this* John Clap, *He was a young old Man, full of Grace, tho' not full of Days.*]

EXAMPLE II.

MR. *Thomas Thornton*, the aged and faithful Pastor of *Yarmouth*, was blessed with a Daughter named *Priscilla*, who at the Age of Eleven, left this World, having first given Demonstrations of an exemplary Piety.

She was one remarkably grave, devout, serious; very inquisitive about the Matters of Eternity; and in her particular Calling very diligent. She was nevertheless troubled with sore Temptations and Exercises about the State of her own Soul: The Anguish of her Spirit, about her *Body of Death*, caused her to pour out many Tears and Prayers; and she pressed, That some other pious Children of her Acquaintance, might with her keep a Day of Humiliation together, *That* (as she expressed it) *they might get Power against their sinful Natures.* But it pleased God at length to bless the Words of her godly Mother, for the quieting of her

[...]ind. It was her singular Happiness, that [sh]e had such godly Parents; but it was her [o]pinion and Expression, *We trust too much to [th]e Prayers of our Parents, whereas we should [pr]ay for our selves.*

At last, she fell mortally sick. In the Be[gi]nning of her Sickness, she was afraid of dy[in]g; *For,* said she, *I know of no Promise to en[co]urage me.* She could not but own that she [ha]d in some Measure walked with God; yet [sh]e complain'd, That she had not found God [m]eeting her in her Prayers, and making her [h]eart willing to be at his dispose; and that [th]e *Pride* of her Heart now lay as a Load upon [her]. She own'd, That she had many Tho'ts of [J]esus Christ, and that it grieved her that she [h]ad sinned against him, who had *done* and *dy'd* [fo]r her.

But many Days were not past, before she [w]ould profess herself *willing to die,* with some [A]ssurance of her then going to eternal Blessed[n]ess. Many Thanks and Loves did she now [re]nder to one of her Superiors, declaring, *[it] was because they had curb'd her, and restrain[ed] her from sinful Vanities.* And she said, *[W]ere I now to choose my Company, it should be [am]ong the People of God; I see plainly that they [ar]e the only Company.* She was not without [he]r Conflicts in this Time, wherein one of her [sp]eeches was, *Damnation, that is the worst [th]ing of all, but Christ is of all the best: I find [it] so; Christ is to me Wisdom, Righteousness,*

Sanctification and Redemption. She told her Father she knew she was made up of all Manner of Sin; but said she, *I hope God has humbled me, and pardoned me in the Merits of the Lord Jesus Christ.* Unto her affectionate Mother she said, *Mother, why do you weep, when I am well in my Soul? Will you mourn, when I am so full of Joy? I pray rejoice with me.*

When she was extreamly spent, she said unto her Parent, *O my Father, I have been much troubled by Satan, but I find Christ is too hard for him, and Sin, and all.* She now said, *I know now that I shall die;* and being asked, Whether she were afraid of Death; with a sweet Smile she replied, *No not I, Christ is better than Life.* And so she continued in a most joyful Frame, till she died: a little before which, it being the Lord's Day, she asked, What Time of the Day it was? and when they had told her, 'Twas three of the Clock, she replied, *What is the Sabbath almost done? Well, my Eternal Sabbath is a going to begin, wherein I shall enjoy all Felicity, and sing Hallelujahs to all Eternity.* And hereupon she quickly fell asleep in the Lord.

EXAMPLE III.

MR. NATHANAEL MATHER, died *October* 17, 1688, at the Age of Nineteen, an Instance of more than common Learning and Virtue. On his Grave-Stone at *Salem,* there are these Words deservedly inscribed, THE ASHES OF AN HARD STUDENT, A GOOD SCHOLAR, AND A GREAT CHRISTIAN.

He was one, who used an extraordinary Diligence to obtain Skill in the several Arts that make an Accomplished *Scholar* ; but he was more diligent in his Endeavours to become an experienced *Christian*.

He did with much of Solemnity enter into COVENANT with GOD, when he was about Fourteen Years old. And afterwards he renewed that solemn Action, in such a Form as this ;

'I do Renounce all the Vanities and wretch-
' ed Idols and evil Courses of the World.

' I do choose, and will ever have, the great GOD, for my best Good, my last End, my only Lord. He shall be the only One, in the glorifying and enjoying of whom shall be my Welfare ; and in the serving of whom shall be my Work.

' I will ever be rendring unto the Lord
' Jesus Christ, my proper Acknowledgments,
' as unto my Priest, my Prophet, and my King,
' and the Physician of my Soul. I will ever
' be studying what is my Duty in these Things,
' and wherein I find my self to fall short, I will
' ever count it my Grief and Shame ; and be-
' take my self to the Blood of the everlast-
' ing Covenant.

' Now humbly imploring the Grace of the

'Mediator to be sufficient for me, I do as a
'further Solemnity, hereunto subscribe my
'Name, with both Heart and Hand.

Having done this, he did for the rest of his Life walk with Watchfulness and Exactness.

One of the *Directories*, which he drew up for himself, was This;

'O that I might lead a *spiritual Life!*
'Wherefore let me regulate my Life by the
'*Word* of God, and by such Scriptures as these,

'1. For regulating my *Thoughts*, Jer. 4. 14.
'Isai. 55. 7. Psal. 104. 34.

'2. For regulating my *Affections*, Col. 3.
'2, 5. Gal. 5. 24. For my *Delight*, Psal. 1. 2.
'For my *Joy*, Phil. 4. 4. My *Desire*, Isai. 2. 6.
'8. 9. My *Love*, Matth. 22. 37. My *Hatred*,
'Psal. 97. 10. My *Fear*, Luk. 12. 4. 5. My
'*Hope*, Psal. 39. 7. My *Trust*, Psal. 62. 8.
'Isai. 26. 4.

'3. For regulating my *Speech*, Eph. 4. 29.
'Col. 4. 6. Deut. 6, 6, 7.

'4. For regulating my *Work*, Tit. 3. 8.
'1. Tim. 5. 10. Mat. 5. 47.

Another of his *Directories* was form'd into into an *Hymn*.

'Lord, What shall I return unto
'Him from whom all my Mercies flow?
   '(I.) To me to live, it CHRIST shall be,
'For all I do I'll do for *Thee*.
   '(II.) My Question shall be oft beside,
'*How thou mayst most be glorify'd.*
   '(III.) I will not any Creature love;

'But in the Love of Thee above.
  '(IV.) Thy Will I will embrace for mine;
'And every Management of thine
'Shall please me. (V.) A Conformity
'To Thee, shall be my Aim and Eye.
  '(VI.) Ejaculations shall ascend
'Not seldom from me (VII.) I'll attend
'Occasional Reflections and
'Turn all to Gold that comes to Hand.
  '(VIII.) And in particular among
'My Cares I'll try to make my *Tongue*,
'A *Tree of Life*, by speaking all
'As be accuntable who shall.
  '(IX.) But *last*, nay *first* of all, I will
'Thy Son my Surety make and still,
'Implore Him, that he would me bless,
'With Strength as well as Righteousness.

He would also keep *whole* Days of Prayer and Praise by himself: And he would set himself to consider much on that Question, *What shall I do for God?*

He was much in *Meditation*, and often wrote the chief Heads of his Meditation. He would read the Scripture, with a *Note* and a *Wish* fetched out of every Verse: And at Night, he would ask,

1. *What has God's Mercy to me been this Day?*
2. *What has my Carriage to God been this Day?*
3. *If I die this Night, is my immortal Spirit safe?*

Many more such imitable Things are in the History of his Life (divers Times printed at *London*) reported of him.

EXAMPLE IV.

ANN GREENOUGH, the Daughter of of Mr. *William Greenough*, left the World, when she was but about five Years old, and yet gave astonishing Discoveries of a Regard unto GOD and CHRIST, and her own Soul, before she went away. When she heard any Thing about the Lord Jesus Christ, she would be strangely transported, and ravished in her Spirit at it; and had an unspeakable Delight in *Catechising*. She would put strange *Questions* about eternal Things, and make *Answers* her self that were extreamly pertinent. Once particularly, she asked, *Are not we dead in Sin?* and presently added, *But I will take this away, the Lord Jesus Christ shall make me alive.* She was very frequent and constant in *secret Prayer*, and could not with any Patience be interrupted in it. She told her gracious Mother, *That she there prayed for her!* And was covetous of being with her Mother, when she imagined such Duties to be going forward. When she fell sick at last of a Consumption, she would not by any sports be diverted from the Tho'ts of *Death*, wherein she took such Pleasure, that she did not Care to hear of any Thing else. And if she were asked, *Whether she were willing to die?* She would chearfully reply, *Ah, by all Means, that I may go to the Lord* Jesus Christ.

EXAMPLE V.

AT *Boston*, 12 d. 3 m. 1694, there died one DANIEL WILLIAMS, in the Eighteenth Year of his Age.

There was a Collection made of some of his dying Speeches.

Being asked, *Whether he loved God?* He replied, *Yes, I love him dearly; for Lord, whom have I in Heaven but Thee?*

He said, ' God hath promised, *They that seek him Early shall find Him* : Ever since I was
' a Child, I dedicated my self to seek and serve
' the Lord. Tho' I have not had so much
' Time as others, yet that little Time which I
' had, I spent in waiting on, and wrestling
' with God by Prayer; and I said, *I will not let Thee go, 'till thou hast blessed me.*

Seeing some of his Relations weep, he said *Why do you cry, when I am ready to sing for Joy?*

They saying, They knew not how to part with him, he replied, *Are you not willing I should go to my heavenly Father? I shall quickly be with my heavenly Father, and with his holy Angels, where they are singing of Hallelujahs. It's better being there than here. When I am there, I shan't wish my self here, in this troublesome World again. I have a Desire to depart, and be with Christ, which is best of all.*

He was much concerned for poor perishing Souls. He would say, ' Oh, that I had but
L.

'Strength! How would I Pray, and Sigh, and Cry to God, for the poor World, that lives in Sin and Pride!'

He expressed himself most pathetically to his Relations, when he took his Leave of them.

At last, he asked, *What Angel that was, that he saw before him? Well,* said he, *I shall quickly be with him: Come, Lord Jesus, come quickly!*

A Friend asking how he did, he said, '*I am one bound for Heaven.* I would not have you pray for my Life; I am afraid you do!'

On the Day of his Death, being full of Pain, he said, 'Jesus Christ bore more than this, and he died for me; and shall I be afraid to die, and go to Him:'

Then said he, *O Death, where is thy Sting? O Grave, where is thy Victory?*

EXAMPLE VI.

An Extract of a Letter from Southold, 23d. 4 m. 1698.

'I Have been requested, to give you this Account from the Parents of a gracious Child, who in all her Life did comport herself to walk in the Lord's holy Fear, and gave a great Attention in hearing the Word of God, and the Lord was pleased to ripen her for Himself, tho' she was but fifteen Years and four Months old. Tho' she was Young, it pleased the Lord to put a great Fear and Awe upon her Heart of breaking the *fifth*

' Commandment. And when she was under the
' Dispensation of God in Sickness, it pleased
' the Lord for to endue her with Patience, to
' be willing to bear his Hand with all Meek-
' ness. She confessed her self to be a great
' Sinner, and to have sinned against a graci-
' ous God. But the Lord vouchsafed her a
' strong Faith, to believe that he is a merci-
' ful God, and willing to forgive Sins, and
' that he had forgiven her Sins, in the Blood
' of our blessed Saviour Jesus Christ. And,
' therefore she was very willing to leave the
' World, and her Father and Mother, having
' Faith that she was going to Christ: These
' were her own Expressions. When her
' Mother did ask her, if she was *willing to die*,
' for she was *too young to die*: She sometime
' before she died, said, she was not *fit to die*,
' but prayed unto the Lord, that he would
' please to *fit* her and make her willing to die.
' Oh, said she, *Death comes unawares, it comes*
' *like a Thief in the Night!* The Lord granted
' her Desire: For afterwards, when her Mo-
' ther asked her, *My Child are you willing to*
' *die*, Her Answer was, That now she was *will-*
' *ing to die*, and leave a thousand Worlds, and
' Father and Mother and all to go to Christ.
' She desired that the Curtains might be drawn,
' that the Light of this World might not de-
' prive her from beholding the Brightness and
' the Glory of the other World. And when
' she see her Father and Mother weeping for

' her, she said, *My dear Father and Mother,*
' *don't mourn for me; you might well mourn for*
' *me, if I were to go into utter Darkness; but I*
' *am going to God in Heaven.* I long to be in the
' New Jerusalem, with the Lord Jesus Christ:
' And now I can die. And lying a while in an
' Agony, when she came out of that Agony,
' she said, *Mother, did you not hear me sing. I*
' *thought I was in Heaven with the Lord Jesus*
' *Christ, and my Grand Parents, and the holy*
' *Angels, and heard such melodious Praises of*
' *God, as I never heard; and I was very sorry*
' *I colud not sing like them.* She said unto her
' Relations, *Oh, don't set your Hearts upon the*
' *World, nor look for the Honours and Riches of*
' *this World; but seek first the Kingdom of*
' *Heaven!* She would call upon her Father to
' go to Prayer at the Even, and say, *I cannot,*
' *I dare not go to sleep without it.* She wish-
' ed, That some young People might come to
' her, to put 'em in Mind to *consider their lat-*
' *ter End,* and leave off their Pride. There
' came a young Maid to see her, and she said
' to her with Tears, that she should not follow
' the Fashions of the World, and not put off
' Repentance to a sick Bed. Yea, she spake
' to all them that were about her, *That they*
' *would not mind this World, but the other World.*
' Her Mother asked her, if she was not afraid
' to lie in the Dust? But she was not tho'tful,
' what should become of her Body, believing
' her Soul should go to God. *Mother,* said

'she, *I could not sing here, but now I am going*
'*to sing the Praises of God in Heaven.* Look-
'ing on her Father she said, *Oh, Father, there*
'*is no God like our God, for he is a God pardon-*
'*ing Iniquity, Transgression and Sin.* She said,
'*I wonder how you do to love to live in such a*
'*troublesome evil and sinful World: Don't you*
'*see how the Judgments of God, are all over the*
'*Earth.* She often cried out, *O Lord Jesus,*
'*Come: Let thine Angels come, and carry me to*
'*the Bosom of Abraham.*

'This is a true Relation of this gracious
'Flower of the Lord Jesus Christ: She was
'an only Child; her Name was *Bethiah*, the
'Daughter of *Thomas* and *Mary Longworth.*

'The Lord raise up your Heart, to declare
'his wonderful Mercies, in working so graci-
'ously upon the Heart of such a young Flow-
'er; that the Lord may raise up more such
'gracious Souls in our rising Generation.

I remain,
Your affectionate Brother,

J. S.

EXAMPLE VII.

A notable Passage, transcribed from the Life of
Mr. John Baily, *as it was related in a Ser-
mon preached on the Day of his Funeral at
Boston. By Dr.* COTTON MATHER.

'FRom a Child he did know the holy Scrip-
'tures: Yea, From a Child he was wise

' *unto Salvation!* In his very *Childhood* he dif-
' covered the *Fear of God* upon his young
' Heart, and *Prayer to God* was one of his
' early Exercises.

' There was one very remarkable Effect of
' it. His *Father* was a Man of a very licen-
' tious Conversation; a Gamester, a Dancer,
' a very lewd Company keeper. The Mother
' of this *Elect Vessel*, one Day took him
' while he was yet a *Child*; and calling the
' Family together, made him to *pray* with
' them. His *Father* coming to understand at
' what a Rate the *Child* had prayed with his
' Family, it smote the Soul of him with a
' great Conviction, and proved the Beginning
' of his Conversion unto God. God left not
' off working on his Heart, until he proved
' one of the most eminent Christians in all that
' Neighbourhood. So he *lived*, so he *died*;
' a Man of more than ordinary Piety. And
' it was his Manner sometimes to retire unto
' those very Places of his Lewdnesses, where
' having that his little Son in his Company,
' he would pour out Floods of Tears in repent-
' ing Prayers before the Lord.

EXAMPLE VIII.

Of Daniel Bradly, *the Son of* Nathan Hester
Bradly, *of* Guilford, *Connecticut, New-England.*

WHEN the said Child was about three
Years old, he had one Night an Impression of the Fears of Death, which put him

; his Mother told him, if he died
o to Heaven; unto which he renew not how to like that Place,
ould be acquainted with no Body.
, upon all Occasions, he was inqui-
t the State of Souls after Death,
to have real Apprehensions about
; unto it, if not beyond his Capacity.
d Day Ague took him in his sixth
eld him near three Years: Some
ore his Death he had many grie-
in which his Patience was very ob-
et he once felt a Pang of Impati-
o think it had been better he had
jorn, yet submitted to his Father's
fter which he began to be assaulted
the Fears of Death, and manifest-
Conceptions about the World to
could not see God, nor could he
ow he should love God better than
nor how God should love him,
could live in Heaven, especially if
were not there, or if he might not

He also expressed Difficulty to
Resurrection of the Body, and was
asking his Mother Questions about
his Nature, and how it could be,
and was eaten up of Worms, he
;ain: she then told him the Words
*d though after my Skin Worms de-
dy, yet in my Flesh shall I see God*:
old him any Thing that she heard,

or the good People so happrehended, or the like, it gave him little Content, except she could assure him it was so in the Bible; and that would always set him down quiet. He told his Mother, that he thought the Reason why People read in the Bible, was that they might find out what God would have them to do; and they prayed for what they would have God do for them. He was much troubled that he was not beg enough to pray; his Father told him that Parents prayed for their Children; but that did not satisfy him, 'till it was told him he was big enough to pray for himself; but then he doubted he could not pray aright: His Mother told him he must pray according to his Ability, and GOD would accept it: Then he addressed himself to the Duty, and would have all go out of the Room except his Mother, and she to stay; that if he prayed what was not right, she might tell him; then with great Solemnity he fixed his Eyes, and asked his Mother whether he should begin with that Expression (BLESSED GOD) which was not usual in the Beginning of Prayer in his hearing, and he manifesting some extraordinary realising Apprehensions of God, was exceeding affecting to his Mother. The Substance of his Prayer was, *That he might live and be a Comfort to his Parents; or if he must die, that God would own him, and love him, and help him to love God, and make him know how it should be with him in the World to come; and defired to be willing to die when his Time come.* After this he frequently was obferved to pray, and defired to be alone for that End. One Time he had a great Sadnefs fell upon him, that lafted fome Time before the Caufe of it was known: But at laft he told his Mother, God was always angry with him, and he was afraid to tell her why, till fhe perfwaded him; then he confeffed, that he had been guilty of a Lie that he told, and fhould have told another, if he had not fome Way been prevented, and that he doubted the Sin of that to him was as great as if he went thro' with it: His Mother afked him, if he were forry for it; he faid he was formerly forry for it, but now more than ever; his Mother told him, if he were forry for it, God would have Mercy: He afked her whether it were fo in the Bible; fhe told him, the Word was, *He that confeffeth and forfaketh his Sin, fhall find Mercy:* He faid, he knew what confeffing was, but he did not underftand forfaking; fhe faid, it was to do fo no more, that gave him fome quiet: yet ftill Trouble and fear of God's Anger hung about him: Then his Mother told him of Chrift's Redemption, and of his Sins being pardoned, thro' him, and our Need of an Intereft in that Redemption; at which he fmiling and wondering afked, Whether it was certainly fo, that Chrift died for Man's fake; he faid, He had never heard it before. She afked, If he did not remember it had been read in the Family, or taught in the Catechism? He said he did not, but now greatly rejoyced in the Apprehension of Christ's Love so revealed.

After this he had a strong Pang of Temptation, and asked his Sister, whether she might not kill him? His Mother (being out of the Room) came in, and reproved him for saying so sinful a Word. He asked her how it appeared to be Sin, seeing he lived in so much Pain: She put him in Mind of Mr. *Cotton*'s Explication of the sixth Command, *that we are not to shorten the Lives of our selves, or others, but preserve both*; (upon which he paused a while;) and then desired his Mother to teach him the Catechism (which he had learnt before) and she did from the Beginning, until she came past that Question of the sixth Command, which he readily answered to; but then desired to go to that which was better. She asked him, what he meant? He answered, where-about it speaks of the eternal Son of God: she turned to that Part of the Catechism, and upon that Answer, *Jesus Christ is the only Son of God, who for our sakes became Man, that he might redeem and save us.* He lifted up his Hand, and said, *It is enough*, and so seemed to meditate thereon.

Also it was observed, that before and after his Sickness began, that he hath so dealt with and reproved grown Persons, for what in them he saw was Evil (in private) that the Persons themselves have confessed, that they hoped his

Christian Reproofs would be for their Good, that they should never forget them, for in them he did speak to their Consciences.

He had a Desire to make a Will, to dispose of what he had, that he might leave it as a Token of his Love to his Relations, and other of his Friends he had received Kindness from in his Sickness; but would not do it, until he had his Father's Consent, which he desired; the which being granted, he disposed of those Things he had (tho' some of them were but Trifles) with as much Discretion and prudent Consideration as if they had been Matters of the greatest Moment, and he a Man of mature Judgment. Ordered also who would dig his Grave; expressed his desire to die, and was heard praying for Death; and told his Mother immediately before he died, he was now going to Heaven, and that it would be best for her, that he should die, for now she was forced to take a great deal of Pains with him, but then she should be at Rest; asked her, if she did not see it was so, and wondred at her slowness to acknowledge it; remembred his Love to his Relations, thankful to those that had been often Watching with him, and prayed his Mother to remember them all with such Tokens of his Love, as were in his Power to give, nominating several particular Persons; and all this he spake with great Chearfulness, and yet with Solemnity; and so sunk down in his Mother's Arms, and died quietly.

Early PIETY Exemplified in *Elizabeth Butcher*.

SECTION I.

Containing a brief Account of her, from her Birth in July 1709, to her first *Remarkable Illness in September 1716.*

1. ELIZABETH BUTCHER, Daughter of *Alvin* and *Elizabeth Butcher* of *Boston*, was born *July* 14th 1709. Her Parents gave her up to God from the Womb, and as soon as she was capable of speaking, they began to instruct her in the Things of God.

2. When she was about *Two Years and half Old*; as she lay in the Cradle, she would ask her self that Question, *What is my corrupt Nature?* and would make Answer again to her self, *It is empty of Grace, bent unto Sin, and only to Sin, and that continually.* She took great Delight in learning her Catechism, and would not willingly go to Bed without saying some Part of it.

3. She being a weakly Child, her Mother carried her into the Country for Health: And when she was about *Three Years* old, and at Meeting, she would set with her Eyes fix'd on the Minister, to the Admiration of all that sat about her, who said that grown up People might learn and take Example of her. She

took great Delight in reading, and was ready and willing to receive Instruction.

4. But nothing more extraordinary as we remember appeared in her, till she came to be about *Six Years* old. Then she began to inquire concerning God, and the Nature and Affairs of her Soul, and she said, *She was afraid she had not lived up to that End for which she was made.* She was asked what was the End she was made for? The Child answered—*To glorify God: But I am afraid I have not lived to the Glory of God as I should have done.* She was told that she must pray to God that He would please to pardon her Sins, and give her Grace to serve and glorify Him.

5. She was not contented with the bare reading of God's Word, but would frequently ask the meaning of it. And when she was at her Work, she would often ask where such and such Places of Scripture were, and would mention the Words that she might be directed to find them.

6. It was her Practice to carry her Catechism or some other good Book to Bed with her, and in the Morning she would be sitting up in her Bed reading before any of the Family were awake besides her.

7. One Day as she was sitting by the Fire, ask'd—*Why our first Parents eating the forbidden Fruit was counted Sin to them?* At an other Time she ask'd, *Who were meant by the wise*

and *foolish Virgins? And what was meant by the Oyl in the Lamps?* As she was reading a Sermon of Dr. *Cotton Mather*'s she ask'd, *Who was meant by the goodly Cedar?* And when she was told, she said,---*And who are meant by the Fowls that are just Fledged?* she was told they meant little Children; and Christ called them to come to Him. But, said she, *How can I who am but a Child go to Christ?* Being informed, she said,----*But will Christ accept of me?* She was answered Yes, and several Places of Scripture were mentioned for her Encouragement.

Section II.
Containing a short Account of her in her first Illness from Sept. 1716. *to* Feb. 1716-17.

1. IN *September* 1716, she was taken Ill, and in her Sickness behav'd her self with such wonderful Patience as all that came near admir'd. She would often put up that Request, *Heavenly Father, Give me thy Christ, give me thy Grace, and Pardon all my Sins, for Jesus Christ's Sake, Amen.* Then she said, *What is Sanctification?* And made Answer to her self; *It is the Work of God's free Grace.---What are the Benefits which in this Life do accompany or flow from Justification, Adoption and Sanctification? They are Assurance of God's Love, Peace of Conscience, Joy in the Holy Ghost, Increase of Grace, and Perseverance therein to the End.*

2. Being ask'd, if she was willing to die, and go to Christ; she said, *Yes:* But Child you

know you are a Sinner; she said *Yes:* And you know where the Wicked go when they die; she said, *Yes, they are cast into Hell*: And being asked, if she was not afraid of going thither: she said, *No, for Christ is an all-sufficient Saviour, and He is able to save me, and I hope he will: Tho' I have not yet seen Christ, yet I hope I shall see him.*

3. A while after she said, *I am weary of this World, and long to be gone? O when shall I go, O when shall I go!* Her Mother asked her if she was willing to leave her here alone? She answered, *Yes, For when you die I hope you will go to Heaven too.*

4. She feeling an Alteration in her self, desired her Mother to send for Mr. *Sewall*; and when he came, he asked her, how she did; she answered, *Very weak:* He ask'd her if she was willing to die? she said, *Yes:* He said, do you not know you are a Sinner? *Yes:* He ask'd her, If she had not heard that there was another and a better World than this? she answer'd, *Yes.* He asked her several other Questions, but they slipt my Memory. He was a going to ask her one Question, but said it was a great one to ask a Child, but however he wou'd, and said to her, Child, are you willing humbly to submit to the Will of God either for Life or Death? she said *Yes.*

5. A while after she was weeping, and being asked the Reason, she said, *I tho't I saw the Flames of Hell and was going there, but I th't*

I saw Christ, and He call'd me to come to Him; and then I was not afraid; and I have cried to God for Grace to serve Him.

6. A while after she was taken with Convulsion Fits, and lay several Hours, all Hopes of Recovery being taken away: But she reviving again, her Pain returned with greater Violence: she prayed to God to take her away out of this miserable World, and cried,—*O God, my God, if thou wilt please to take me away, I will be willing to bear what Pain thou shalt please to lay upon me: O God, my dear God, I love Thee dearly!* And this she repeated several Times over.

7. Her Mother sitting by her weeping, the Child said, *Dear Mother, you make me have more Pain:* Her Mother said, No, my dear Child I don't: She said, *Yes, you cry, and that troubles me, and causes me to have more Pain.*

8. Mr. *Sewall* being sent for again, He said, Child, Is it not better to be in Heaven with God and Christ, than to be here? She answered, *Yes, Yes.* He ask'd her if he should pray to God that He would be pleas'd to take her to Himself? She made a quick Reply, doubling her Words, *Yes, Yes.* He asked her another Question, but being in great Trouble it slipt my Memory: But the Child made no Answer to it, and only said, *I am spent.*

9. A few Hours After, her Pains abating again, the Fits returned with more Violence than before, and held her several Hours, and then left her. She lay for some Days so sense-

less that she knew not those that came to see her. But it pleased God to restore her again to her former Health: And before she was able to sit up, she would call for her Book and lie and read by the Hour together.

SECTION III.

Containing a brief Account of her from her First *remarkable* Illness *in the Fall and Winter,* 1716, *to her* second, *in* April 1718.

1. SHE had by Course read almost thro' the *Old Testament*; but at other Times her Delight was to read in the *New*, concerning the Birth of Christ and his Sufferings; and would ask the meaning of what she read.

2. One Day as she sat by her self reading the 7th of the *Revelations* concerning the Number of them that were sealed; when she came to the 9th *Verse*, she was overheard to weep till she came to the *End* of the *Chapter*.

3. One Morning as she lay in her Bed, she asked, *what was meant by the Fountain, and the House of David, and the Inhabitants of Jerusalem,* in Zech. 13. 1.

4. Hearing a Sermon from *Luke* 15. concerning the Prodigal Son; a few Days after, she was saying the Text over to herself; she then ask'd, *Who was meant by the Father? and who by the Son?*

5. She had begun to learn the Proofs of the Assemblies Catechism: and when she came to that in, 1 *Joh.* 5. 7. She asked, *If the Father*

M 2

was God, and if the Son was God also, and if the Holy Ghost was God also? For it is said here, That there a Three that bear Record in Heaven, the Father, the Word and the Holy Ghost, and these Three are One : *And this seems as if there were Three Gods, and yet there is but One.* And she desired to be told something of this Mystery. She was told, There was but One GOD, tho' there were Three Persons in the Godhead. That Christ was the Eternal Son of God, and the same in Substance and equal with the Father in Power and Glory, and was God. Then said the Child, *Tho' Christ be the Son of God, Yet He is God also?* Answer was made her, Yes: and that the Holy Ghost was the Spirit of God, and proceeded both from the Father and the Son, and was the same in Substance with Them both, and was equal in Power and Glory. And a while after she ask'd, *If Christ took upon Him the Nature of a Man?* She was told that He did.

1. She rejoiced greatly when the *Lord's Day* came, especially if it were fair Weather for her to go to the Publick Worship of God. And when she came Home, she would take a Book and sit and Read, till it was time to go to the Afternoon Exercise, without the least Sign of Weariness. And if she was detained at Home on the *Sabbath*; she would not spend the Day in Idleness, but in Religious Imployments.

7. It pleased God to exercise her with great Pain in every Part of her Body, which did

something impair the Natural Quickness and Strength of her Senses. But between *Two or Three Months* before her Death, her Understanding was brighten'd to Admiration.

8. When the *Spring* came on, and mention was made of the Publick Catechizing; she Rejoyced greatly and would be often Speaking of its Drawing near. One Morning as she lay in her Bed she said; *O that Charming Day, O that sweet Day is coming!* Being asked, What Day she meant? She answer'd, *Catechizing-Day, I mean that sweet Day.* A few Days after she said, *I won't depend upon going to Catechizing, For I believe I shall be prevented by some Means or other.* She was told, If she was well and the Weather permitted, nothing else wou'd hinder her. *Ah!* said the Child, *I am Perswaded I shall be prevented some way or other from going.* And according to the strong Impulse she had upon her mind, it proved to her: For she was taken Sick *Two or Three Days* before the Catechizing came, which was in *April* 1718.

SECTION IV.

Containing a more Particular Account of her in her Second Illness, from April 1718. *to* June *Succeeding, when She Died.*

1. WHEN she was First taken, she was in some Doubt of her Spiritual State, and said, *She was afraid she did not belong to God, nor Love Him as she should; For Mother, You have told me, That they that Fear God and Love*

Him, make it their chief Care and Endeavour to keep his Commandments: But I am afraid I have not kept them as I ought. Her Mother ask'd her, What particular Command she cou'd accuse her self of Breaking: She said, *The Fifth Commandment faith, Honour thy Father and thy Mother; and have I Honoured You? Have I obeyed you as I ought.* Her Mother told her; You have been an Obedient Child to me, and wherein you have offended in any small Matter, I do forgive you and Pray God to Forgive you also.

2. The Day following she cryed out, *I am a great Sinner, a great Sinner, What will become of me, Oh what will become of me! I am afraid that God will not have Mercy on me, My Sins are so many and so great.* She was told, Tho' her Sins were ever so great and many, yet the Mercy of God was greater and more abundant than her Sins; For that was like Himself Infinite, and endureth for ever, That there was Forgiveness with Him that He might be Feared, and He had Promised, That those who Confess, and Forsake their Sins should find Mercy. But said the Child, *Satan tempts me to Despair of Mercy, because my Sins are so great and many.* But she was then Exhorted not to give way to the Temptations of Satan, but to Hope in the Mercy of God; For the Lord taketh Pleasure in them that Fear Him, and in them that Hope in His Mercy. And she was told that He say'd in *Isa.* 55. 7. Let the wick-

ed forsake his way, and the unrighteous Man his thoughts, and let him return unto the Lord, and He will have Mercy upon him, and to our God; for He will abundantly Pardon.

3. A while after she said, *Behold I was shapen in Iniquity, and in Sin did my Mother conceive me: I am a Miserable and Sinful Creature: Convinced I am of Sin, but afraid not Converted: I am a Poor Creature that has no sight of my Interest in Christ, and without a Christ, without a Christ, I am undone for ever: Oh for a Christ, Oh for a Christ, for a Christ to Save me!* And then she Prayed and said.----

4. *LORD, Have Mercy on me according to thy Loving Kindness: according to the Multitude of thy Tender Mercies blot out all my Transgressions with thine own Blood: Wash me thro'ly from mine Iniquities, and cleanse me from my Sins. Create in me a clean Heart, O God, and Renew a right Spirit within me: O Give me a new Heart, a humble Heart, a broken Heart, and a contrite Spirit: Oh Sanctify me by thy Holy Spirit thro' out, in Soul, Spirit, and Body: Renew me in the whole Man after thine own Image in Knowledge, Righteousness and true Holiness: Oh Give me a Christ, Give me thy Grace, Pardon all my Sins: O Lord, Take away all mine Iniquity, and Receive me graciously, Circumcise my Heart to Fear thy Name, and Lead me in the way that is pleasing in thy sight: Oh be my God in Life, my Guide unto Death, and the unchangeable Portion of my Soul for ever: Fit and prepare me for all*

Changes, but especially for Death t
Last Change. And this I beg for
Christ's sake, Amen.

5. In the Time of her Health
careful of her Words, and no i
was ever heard to proceed from her
now in her Sickness, she examin'd
Sins she had been Guilty of, bot
& Actions. And taking a View
mandments, some of them she said
fraid she had been guilty of Break
accuse herself of Disobedience, and
her self for her Sins. And being i
of Body; she said, *Now am I suff*
fert of my Sins: Oh that I might
Moments Ease: But I need not w
have no Ease, for I deserve none: Hav
me O Lord, for I am weak O Lord
my Bones are sore vexed: Look upon
on and my Pain, and forgive all my

6. Mr. *Prince* came in to see h
sired him to pray with her: He ask
he should pray for? She answer'd
would be pleas'd to pardon all her Si
her an Interest in *Christ*.

7. A while after she cried out,
poor Creature that wants Assurance:
surance, Oh for Assurance! O that
be pleas'd to lift up the Light of his
upon me! Oh that he wou'd be pleas'
in his Covenant, and bless me. Her
ing her in this Distress, ask'd her if

[143]

Sewall to talk with him, and hear
to say to her? The Child answer-
all may give me Incouragement as
except God speaks to me too, all will
g. Well Child, said her Mother,
God still, who will in his own Time
Peace to thy Soul. Mr. *Sewall*
, but he was not at Home.

s told for her Incouragement, That
mb of Christ's Flock; and that he
would take the Lambs in his Arms,
m in his Bosom; and suffer little
come unto me, and forbid them
uch is the Kingdom of Heaven;
w that Promise in *Prov.* 8. 17. I
at love me, and those that seek
ll find me. The Child answered;
will please to help me, I will seek him.
that the Lord wou'd help her, and
orted to trust in the Free Grace &
od through Christ. Oh said the
willing to accept of Christ, but I
rist is not willing: Answer was
she was willing to accept of Christ,
re Christ was willing to accept of
swered, *I am willing.*

e after she said; *I will venture my*
rist, and if I perish, Lord, it shall be
ain of thy Mercy: For thou hast
t whosoever cometh unto thee, thou
se cast out; O Lord, I desire as I
ome unto thee, and I am sure thou

wilt not cast me off. And she was compos'd for some Time: But Satan assaulted her again in setting her Sins before her; and she cried out, *Oh the Sin of my Nature, (unless my Soul be sprinkled with the Blood of Christ,) is enough to undoe me, were I guilty if no other.*

10. About a *Month* before her Death, on the Sabbath in the Afternoon, she said to her Mother; *Now I have a believing Sight of Christ: Now Christ is mine, and I am his: Oh, how sweet is Christ: Oh he is sweet, he is sweet! And if you did but Taste and feel what I do, you would long to be gone.* Then she said; *Come Lord Jesus, come quickly: Dear Jesus, sweet Jesus, come quickly,* Then she said; *Lord Jesus give me Patience, give me Patience to wait thy Time, for thy Time is the best Time: Lord Jesus give me Patience.*

11. Her Mother sat weeping by her, and to comfort her, the Child said; *Dear Mother, tho' we part now, it will be but a little while before you will follow and come to me: and that will be a happy Meeting for us, to meet at the Right Hand of Christ in the Great Day.* Then she thanked her Mother for the Instructions and Corrections she had given her, and said, *Had it not been for them I might have gone to Hell; but it won't be long now before the blessed Angels will come and carry my Soul to the Bosom of Christ; Oh I long to be gone, I long to be gone to that blessed Place: Sweet Lord Jesus, come quickly.*

12. A while after she said; *My Pain is great*

which I undergo to go to Christ; but not so great as the Pains Christ underwent for me: Oh I wonder, I wonder, that Christ shou'd be so willing to die for me, who am so great a Sinner.

13. Mr. *Sewall* was sent for again; but before he came the Child was so spent with extream Pain and much Speaking, that she was not able to say any Thing to him. In the Night she ask'd the young Woman that watch'd with her, to read the 25th of *Matthew* to her.

14. One Morning she ask'd; 'Where is that Place 'of Scripture? Eat O Friends, Drink, yea Drink a-'bundantly, O beloved.' The Glass standing on the Table, she ask'd to have it turned, and said; 'My 'Glass is almost Run, my Work is almost ended.'

15. On Thursday was three Weeks before her Death, her Mother seeing an Alteration in her, said, My Child is struck with Death. Upon which she replied, 'Is Death come, and am I prepared, am I prepared'? She lay still for some Time, and then said; 'O Death where is thy Sting: O Grave where is thy 'Victory, and what wilt thou gain by this Thing'?

16. There was a Person she had a peculiar Respect for, and desired her Mother when she had Opportunity, to speak to her; for she was afraid she did not consider her Soul and Eternity.

17. The Lord's Day following she said over the 23d Psalm, and when she had concluded it, her Mother ask'd her; if she was not afraid to pass thro' the dark Valley of the Shadow of Death? She answer'd; 'No, for God hath promis'd that he will 'never leave me nor forsake me, neither will he 'suffer me to leave or forsake him.'

18. She lying in great Pain Day and Night, wou'd often say, 'Lord Jesus give me Patience, that I may 'not Dishonour God. She said, Oh if I should be

N

' deceiv'd at last, and deceive others, and they think
' I am Good, Oh how miserable shall I be forever?

19. Her Aunt *Stone* being present, and the Child being in great Pain, and complaining of those about her, for refusing to do something for her, which she found relieved her, but they were fearful of overdoing, she said,—They do not pity me, but I hope Christ pities me, and will prepare a place for me. A little while after, being restless with her pains, she check'd herself, saying,—Why do I complain? Christ endured more than this for me: I wonder how he did to bear it. And a little while after, hearing it thunder; she said, It thunders, I am afraid God will kill me with it; but whether he kills me with that, or with this pain, if I may but go to Christ, it will be well.

20. The Tuesday following Mr. *Sewall* came to see her, and after some Discourse, he ask'd her on what she depended for Salvation? She reply'd, On Christ, and the Promises. He said, well Child, hold fast thy Faith, and still trust in Christ. Then she said, Oh I long to go to that blessed Place. He asked her what blessed Place? She not readily answering, he said, Do you mean Heaven? She answered, Yes: And when he was going away, desired him to remember her in his Prayers: And asked him when we would come again to see her?

21. Two Persons being in the room, they said to one another; this Child has been a Child of affliction all its Days. The Child replied; And it is for my Good.

22. She had another combat with Satan, and said, He would perswade her that Christ was withdrawn from her; and she cried out, Oh what shall I do, Oh what shall I do? I am undone! She said, O Lord, cast me not out of thy Sight: cast me not away from thy Presence, and take not thy holy

Spirit from me : Restore unto me the Joy of thy Salvation, and uphold me with thy free Spirit ; never leave me nor forsake me : But guide me by thy Counsel while here, and afterwards receive me to thine heavenly Kingdom : And this I ask for thy Son Jesus Christ's Sake ; and in testimony of my Desires and Assurance to be heard, I say, *Amen.*

23. She was comforted again in the Night : And the Watcher sitting by her Bed-side, about Midnight, heard her say,

    Yonder, Yonder, up above,
    Sits my Saviour, cloath'd in Love,
    And there's my smiling GOD.

24. She said, she had something to say to Mr. *Sewall* the next Time he shou'd come to see her : And being asked what it was, she said, She would thank him for the many Prayers he put up for her, For God had heard and answered them.

25. At another Time she said concerning Christ ; Why is his Chariot so long a coming ? Why stay so long the Wheels of his Chariot ? For me to stay is Pain ; but to die is Gain.

26. Mr. *Prince* coming to see her the Monday before her Death, she desired him to pray with her : He said, well, and what shall we pray for now ? She replied, That I may have a saving Knowledge of Christ, that God wou'd please to pardon all my Sins, and prepare me for Death my great and last change.

27. The Day following, her Pains abated, and she seemed to be better for 2 or 3 Days ; and no one perceiv'd her to draw near her Change, till a few minutes before she was taken Speechless, the Child said, something choak'd her : Her mother felt of her hands, and finding them in a cold sweat, and her Countenance alter, she said, My Child is a going : Ah Mother, said the Child, So must you as well as I. She said something more ; but her speech

and spirits failing, we could not understand her.

She breath'd her Soul into the Arms of Christ on Friday, the 13th of *June*, 1718, being Eight Years and just eleven Months old.

EXAMPLE X.

MRS. ABIEL GOODWIN, who died at *Boston*, October 3, 1727, in the 20th Year of her Age.——Her Father died a very young Man, but in so uncommon and victorious a manner, that an Account is already published of it in Dr. *Cotton Mather*'s Cælestinus. She was born after the Death of her Father, and for that Cause the Name of *Abiel* (or, *God my Father*) was given her.

This young Person was one, who began *Betimes* to take the yoke of her Saviour upon her ; yea, so much betimes, and with such gracious dawns of Piety, that she knew not the time of her first coming into the Life of GOD. And GOD forbid, that we should rashly pass the Doom of the unregenerate on all who are, and very many of the Newborn, we hope, are so circumstanced.

Under the influences of a pious education, she was from her Childhood used unto the religion of the Closet ; and afraid of doing any thing that the Light of GOD in her young Soul allowed not : And courteous, affable and full of Benignity, ready to do good offices for all about her : accompanied and advantaged with a Discretion which was an agreable varnish upon all.

Her attendance on the Means of Grace was very diligent : Wherein among the rest, she constantly attended the weekly Lectures ; and lamented the Scandal of it, that those precious Opportunities were so shamefully neglected in a City, where a worldly Mind so evidently governed the Inhabitants.

Hereby she came so to live by the Faith of the

Son of God, and of his everlasting Love to her, that the Dread of Death was nobly conquered in her: And in the Year 1721, when the *Small-Pox* carried off so many Hundreds in the City of *Boston*, she declared unto her Widow-Mother, that except God had service for her to do, more particularly in being very helpful to her, she would have chosen then to have left a World, that she saw full of little but Sin and Vanity.

Her Illness began upon her, when she was little more than Sixteen Years of Age, and she was confined unto the House for two Years before she died. Hereby she was prevented from the Execution of a Purpose, that her young Heart was earnestly set upon. Which was to have approached the Holy Table in the Way of the Gospel and of our Churches, and have made her Claim to the Sacrifice of her Saviour, and set her Seal to the Covenant of Salvation, according to his Institution there. She greatly lamented it, that tho' she were so very young she had not publickly done what she had proposed, of giving herself up unto the Lord among his People! But she said, I have done it secretly a Thousand Times; and the Lord has accepted my willing Mind; and what Fault there might be in my Delay, he has assured me, that he has pardoned it. But how earnestly did she urge upon her young Friends, the serious and speedy discharge of their plain Duty, Do this; the Omission whereof does forever, where the Conscience is not seared, make an uneasy Death-Bed.

At length she became confined unto the Bed, for eighteen weeks together, at her Entrance whereof she express'd a strong Belief, that she should find extraordinary Supports provided for her. And she found them; Found them to astonishment.

She was now fallen into an Hydrop[sy?]
on. In this Time, tho' many weari[somes?]
were appointed for her, yet she p[assed?]
Months of Vanity. But she did G[od?]
while, and brought much of the Fruit[s?]
her heavenly Father has been and will [be?]

In these Months, the first Thing tha[t we no-]
tice of, is, the Zeal, Flame and Ardou[r where-with?]
she addressed her lively Exhortations, [to all?]
that visited her; to make haste unto t[he Lord?]
and into a Life of Piety, and make sure [of their?]
hold on eternal Life. She did not ve[ry often de-]
fer her Exhortations of this Importan[ce to old?]
people; for, she said, she did not co[unt it good?]
Manners for her to do the Part of a [Monitor to?]
those who were much older than hers[elf. But to?]
younger People she was inexpressibl[y earnest?]
That they would now, even to Day he[ar the voice?]
of God, and remember their Creator, [and Day of?]
Rest, Give no Sleep to their Eyes, nor [Slumber to?]
their Eye-lids, 'till they had got into t[he Favour?]
of God their Saviour, and yielded the[mselves to?]
the Lord, resolving to be the Lord's. [Blessed?]
Winner of Souls, how sweetly did she [say to them,?]
O come and sit under the Shadow of [this Tree, how?]
sweet, sweet will you find his Fruit u[nto you!?]
Great Numbers of younger People c[ame to her,?]
and she not only very importunately, [but very?]
particularly expostulated with them [about their?]
Delay to make thorough Work of th[eir turning?]
to God, and resort unto the Wings o[f Christ,?]
which was infinitely necessary, in or[der to their?]
dying in safety and with comfort. She [was very?]
by the Hand, vehemently solliciting the[m to come?]
unto the Proposal in the Covenant of [Grace, to?]
sign and engage themselves unto th[e Lord;?]
and would not let go their hand, unti[l they?]

ed unto her, That they did so. She pleaded with some of them; 'GOD spared you in the Time of the great mortality six years ago: He has come twice three years, looking for fruit. But O what fruit has he found upon you.' And some, in whom he saw Things amiss, it was very affecting to see how lovingly, but how faithfully and how solemnly she dispensed reproofs unto them. The Hammers were enongh to have broken Rocks to Pieces.

In this Time, as it sometimes is with Souls that are gitting loose from Flesh, and gotten very far on towards the invisible World, she had some unaccountable Impressions upon her Mind, relating to Things not commonly coming under human cognizance. There were surprizing Instances, not so proper to be now and here spoken of. But there is one I would speak of, because it may be a little subservient unto the main Design which I am now to prosecute.

In her Inculcations of it upon young People, that they would immediately come under the Yoke of their Saviour, and so be prepared for a Death, which they knew not how suddenly it might overtake them: She said, 'Mind what I say; you shall see Sudden Deaths, I say, Sudden Deaths, quickly multiplied among you; and young as well as old shall be reached with them.' It was not long, but a very few Weeks after this Prediction, before she was able to observe; 'Well, there have been 14 sudden Deaths, which you have seen dispensed since my speaking to you; but I am to tell you, there will be many more than these.'

But from this, I cannot but go on, to take notice of the Prospect that her Saviour gave her of the Heaven, that she now saw open to receive her; and the heavenly peace and Joy, which the bright prospect filled her withal.

It was unspeakeably edifying unto us, to see so young a Person, one of Nineteen, so rejoicing in Hope of the Glory of GOD : Yea, rejoicing with a Joy unspeakable and full of Glory.

In this Time, when One, to treat her with a term suiting her Ingenuity, told her, that considering the nature of her Malady, her Condition might be called, a going to Heaven by Water : And that anon she would be able to sing unto her Saviour, that song of the redeemed; He sent from above He took me, He drew me out of many Waters. Her Answer was, 'Water, yea, and if I should go to Heaven by Fire too, I am sure, Heaven would compensate for all the trouble of it. O lovely, lovely, lovely, to be there : How do I long to be there.' Then she would break out, ' O that I had the Wings of a Dove ; then would I fly away unto Him and be at Rest.' And again, ' O why is his Chariot so long a coming ? Why tarry the Wheels of his Chariot ?' But she corrected it, 'I will wait, for He that will come shall come, and will not tarry. And, O what shall I find in Mount Zion, the City of the living GOD, the heavenly *Jerusalem*.'

She said that for some Time, though she knew it would be well with her, yet she was at a loss, and knew not how far her departed Soul would apprehend Things in the other World, which it was now going to. But when her Thoughts were one Day full of Perplexity about the Matter, she tho't she heard a Voice distinctly say to her ; ' Be satisfyed, Thy departing Soul shall immediately pass into a wondrous Glory. Thy poor Body also shall still remain united unto thy Redeemer, and it shall be after some Time restored unto thy Soul, with wondrous Glory ; and therein thou shalt for ever glorify Him who has redeemed thee.' The Scriptures being so set in this Light unto her, she broke forth into Raptures; 'O wonderful; O wonderful; Am I so near unto a wondrous Glory: And this vile Body too united to my Saviour, and regarded by Him;—O Grace; Grace;—O free Grace; O rich Grace; I shall glorify thee for evermore.' It was a frequent Exclamation with her; O the Grace of the glorious Rock of Ages; I have Everlasting Strength in that glorious Rock of Ages;

She said, upon her being ask'd her Choice in the Matter; I had rather die, were it the Will of God, if it were for nothing but This; If I live I shall sin: You know now 'tis natural to Sin; and I had rather die than Sin. But if it be the Will of God that I should live, I am willing to live and suffer any Thing that He shall please to order for me. 'Twill be nothing to what my Saviour suffered for me the chief of Sinners.

She often fell into Fits, which were attended with an Extremity of Pains: But at her first coming out of them, her first Words were usually such as one might have expected from One that had been caught up to Paradise. They were, Hallelujah; Oh! Salvation to our GOD, who sitteth on the Throne, and unto the Lamb. O Blessing and Glory and Honour be unto our GOD for ever and ever!---- She said, O welcome Fits, O welcome Pains, O welcome any Thing that will bring me nearer to Christ! She said, Well, The more I Bear, the more I Love! The more I suffer from the wise and good Hand of my Saviour, the more I love him!—Her Mother wiping the Sweat off her Face; hereupon she said, O my Mother, 'Tis not like the Drops of Blood, which my Saviour shed for me a miserable Sinner. One with some Compassion, saying, Poor Creature! She replied, O don't call me so; I am a Rich Creature; for the Blood of the Son of GOD has cleansed me from all my Sins; and his unsearchable

Riches are mine! Another ufing the Term of Diftrefs'd Creature! fhe faid upon it, No, Say, Happy Creature!

She lay awake with her Eyes clofed a long Time together? And being at length afked, What fhe was a doing? She replied, I am Thinking, Think‑
'ing, What that Heaven is which I am going to.
' Thinking, how they are employ'd in Heaven! I
' now know a little of That.---Thinking, What fhall
' be my firft Word when I come to Heaven.' Being
' afked, What it fhould be? She anfwered, ' What?
' Hallelujah! Hallelujah! O the Free and rich
' Grace which has brought me hither! O my Sa‑
' viour, What, What, fhall I render to Thee!

Coming to fpeak about the matchlefs Glories of her Saviour, fhe faid, ' I have read and heard, His
' Name is Wonderful. O! I did not underftand
' the Meaning of that Word: But now I have fome
' underftanding of it. I heard and read, He is al‑
' together Lovely. O I did not know the Meaning
' of that Word; but now I know fomething of it!

Once a Temptation affaulted her, that a Devil would make a Prey of her departing Soul. But fhe foon anfwered it, and vanquifhed it, and faid: ' No,
' No, my Saviour won't let Satan pluck me out of
' his powerful and merciful Hand. Satan, When
' my Hour comes, my Flight will be too nimble
' for thee.

Hereupon fhe expreffed, in very extraordinary Terms, How welcome her death was become unto her. It came unto her, as one that comes to take off the Yoke on the Jaws, and lay Meat unto the Weary. Being afked, If fhe were not Frightned at it. She replied, ' Frightned, No, my Saviour has
' made it a better Friend unto me, than any I have
' in the world O my Friend, how welcome, how wel‑
' come to me.' The Tolls of the Bells for Funerals,

even transported her, to think what Joys the like Tolls for her would proclaim her to be gone unto. And she sent messages unto some sick people in the Neighbourhood, 'That they should not be afraid 'of dying; but repair to the glorious CHRIST that 'she had repair'd unto: And they should find him 'full of Grace; full of Love; the Comforter that 'should relieve their Souls would not be far from 'them.' She therewithal declared, There was one Word, which the Spirit of GOD had made worth a Thousand Worlds, even that Word, 'Our light 'Affliction here, which is but for a Moment, works 'for us a far more exceeding, and eternal Weight 'of Glory.

But I must now own; That tho' her Hope in her Death, was what appear'd very amiable to me and very delectable, yet there was one Thing that appear'd much more so; and this was, ' Her being ' willing to live.

Tho' she so wished for Death, and had such Assurance that the Hour of her Death would be the best Hour that ever she saw: and tho' the Distemper which Cruciated her, had very much Dolour and Anguish in it, and as and by her Expiration, she was assured of the Lord sending to take her and draw her out of deadly Waters; Yet with a most profound Submission, she was willing to wait GOD's Time for the Deliverance. Her Will was admirably swallowed up in the Will of her GOD; and her Cry continually was, The Will of the Lord be done! How often did she so Comfort her self, ' Heaven, ' Heaven will make Amends for all the Pains that ' I undergo in my Passage to it!' How often did she compose herself: ' If I may do Good unto any ' one Soul by my staying here, or if I do no more ' Good than this, that the Sight of my Pain shall ' teach any to be thankful to GOD for their Health

' and Eafe: This alone will make Am
' my Mifery.' She would often fpeak c
for Chrift, and fay, Oh what a Pleafure
unto her to be Burnt to Death for Him
fering from Chrift, fhe often faid, fhe
them with pleafure, becaufe they came
Any Thing from his Hand, fhe faid,
Pleafure to take it.—Thus Patience ha
Work. Being asked, How fhe did? Sh
'Oh, 'Better and Better.—That is to
'and nigher to Heaven.' A little befo
being asked, Whether her comfort con
faid 'Yes, Oh, More than ever. But I
' that I cannot exprefs the Joy I feel.
' than ever to be gone. You may now
' Death every Minute.' Some of he
were, I have now finifhed the work t
has ordered for me.——So fhe kept w
Mercy-Stroke which anon releafed her

THE END.

www.ingramcontent.com/pod-product-compliance
Lightning Source LLC
Chambersburg PA
CBHW030316170426
43202CB00009B/1023